·ooks a ·e t⁻ be r⁻'ı'ı

RONA MUNRO

Rona was born in Aberdeen and has written extensively for
stage, film, radio and television. Theatre credits include *Little
Eagles* (Hampstead Theatre for the Royal Shakespeare
Company); *Pandas* (Traverse Theatre, Edinburgh); *The House
of Bernarda Alba* (National Theatre of Scotland); *The Dirt
Under the Carpet* (Paines Plough and Òran Mór); *Long Time
Dead* (Paines Plough and Plymouth Theatre Royal);
Strawberries in January (Traverse Theatre, Edinburgh);
Watership Down (stage adaptation for the Lyric Theatre,
Hammersmith); *Mary Barton* (Royal Exchange, Manchester);
The Indian Boy (Royal Shakespeare Company); *Iron* (Traverse
Theatre, winner of the John Whiting Award); *The Maiden Stone*
(Hampstead Theatre and Royal Lyceum Theatre, Edinburgh;
Peggy Ramsay Memorial Award Winner); *Gilt* (co-writer); *Bold
Girls* (Susan Smith Blackburn Award, Evening Standard Most
Promising Playwright Award, Plays International Award,
Critics' Circle and Plays and Players Most Promising
Playwright Award). Rona has written over twenty-five shows
for the touring theatre company The MsFits. Film credits
include *Ladybird Ladybird* directed by Ken Loach
(FilmFour/Parallax Pictures Ltd); *Aimee and Jaguar* (Senator
Film Production). For television, credits include: *Rehab*
(BBC2); *Almost Adult* (Channel 4). Rona wrote five of the plays
in the Stanley Baxter Playhouse series for Catherine Ba''
Ltd/BBC Radio 4.

Rona Munro

IRON

NICK HERN BOOKS

London

www.nickhernbooks.co.uk

A Nick Hern Book

Iron first published in Great Britain in 2002 as a paperback original by
Nick Hern Books Limited, 14 Larden Road, London W3 7ST, in
association with the Traverse Theatre, Edinburgh

Reprinted 2004, 2011 (twice), 2012

Iron copyright © 2002 Rona Munro

Rona Munro has asserted her right to be identified as the author of this
work

Typeset by Country Setting, Kingsdown, Kent CT14 8ES
Printed in Great Britain by Mimeo Ltd, St Ives, Cambs, PE27 3LE

ISBN 978 1 85459 703 8

A CIP catalogue record for this book is available from the British Library

Iron was first performed at the Traverse Theatre, Edinburgh, on 26 July 2002, with the following cast:

JOSIE	Louise Ludgate
FAY	Sandy McDade
GUARD 1	Ged McKenna
GUARD 2	Helen Lomax

Director	Roxana Silbert
Designer	Anthony MacIlwaine
Lighting Designer	Chahine Yavroyan
Sound Designer	Matt Mackenzie

Characters

JOSIE, *twenty-five*

FAY, *forty-five*

GUARD 1, *male, fifty-three*

GUARD 2, *female, twenty-four*

ACT ONE

The sounds of a women's prison just before lockdown. A babble of voices like a school playground, echoing, the thwack of heavy doors slammed, someone shouting, on the verge of madness, talking and laughing pitched over this voice, drowning it out.

GUARD 1 (*roars from offstage*). Lock down! Lock down!

The echoing sound of door after door banging shut. Silence, darkness, lights up on . . .

Waiting room. A small area outside the visitors' room. This is where visitors wait for their names to be called. JOSIE *is sitting here, alone. She seems unperturbed, pleasantly interested in her surroundings. Her clothes are fashionable but very low key. She wears black. She looks very plain and very expensive. She's just waiting, perfectly composed.*

After a moment GUARD 2 *enters, she looks at* JOSIE *for a moment without saying anything.* JOSIE *looks back, she smiles pleasantly.*

GUARD 2. You're here to see Prisoner Black?

JOSIE. That's right.

GUARD 2 (*shaking head*). Never thought I'd see the day . . .

JOSIE. Is there a problem? You didn't call my name.

GUARD 2. So who are you?

JOSIE. Josie . . . Josie Kerr? I'm . . . She was my mother.

Pause. GUARD 2 *is completely flabbergasted.*

GUARD 2. You're her daughter?

JOSIE. Yes.

GUARD 2. Unbelievable.

I'm sorry darling, you don't know what's going on here do you? I've known your Mum the best part of four years you see, see her every day I'm working. I know Fay really well.

JOSIE. Right.

GUARD 2. Same with all the lifers, you know them inside out after a while. Never had a daughter in the picture at all.

JOSIE. Well . . . I've not visited before.

GUARD 2. No-one has. I couldn't believe she had a visitor, let alone a daughter.

JOSIE. No. We haven't been in touch.

GUARD 2. Well don't think I blame you darling. We know. It's hard on families.

Pause.

JOSIE. So can I see her?

GUARD 2. Now you see, I'm not explaining myself am I? You've not done this before.

JOSIE. No. I wasn't sure . . . I rang and checked she was here you know and found out the visiting times . . .

GUARD 2. You can't just turn up. She has to ask to see you.

JOSIE. Oh.

GUARD 2. You didn't know. It's not your fault. What you have to do is write to her you see and say you want to visit, then if she's O.K. with that she asks for a visitor's form and fills it in and then, if that's approved we send you a visitor's pass with the times you can come. That's how it works. It's only fair. If they don't want to see someone they can't get away from them can they? Have to let them have a bit of control there.

JOSIE. Of course. Yes. I see.

GUARD 2. Were you hoping to surprise her?

JOSIE. I suppose I was.

GUARD 2. Just drop in.

JOSIE. I hadn't . . . I suppose I hadn't really thought it through.
I was pretty surprised I wanted to see her to be honest.
Thought I better just go for it.

GUARD 2. No you can't do that. Sorry.

JOSIE. Alright then.

JOSIE *is about to leave*.

GUARD 2. Have you come a long way?

JOSIE. I felt I had to see her.

GUARD 2. 'Cause I tell you what we could do, you could
write a note and I could see she gets it.

JOSIE *hesitates*.

JOSIE. What would I say?

GUARD 2. Tell her you want to visit.

JOSIE. I don't know. I thought I'd do it today.

GUARD 2. Better this way, believe me. A surprise is a great
idea but you never know how it'll work out. We don't like
the unexpected in here, any of us.

JOSIE *still hesitates*.

You worried she might not want to see you?

JOSIE. I didn't think of that.

GUARD 2. You've got nothing to lose though really have you?

JOSIE. I don't know. I suppose not.

GUARD 2. Just write her a note and let her know your address
and everything so she can get back to you.

JOSIE. Right. You see I'm staying in a hotel here.

GUARD 2. Well it takes a while for all the paperwork to come
through. Just put your home address.

JOSIE. Right. You see I'm sort of homeless right now.

GUARD 2. Well you're not sleeping in a ditch are you?

JOSIE. I don't know where I'm sleeping to be honest.

GUARD 2. Oh . . . well as long as you've got a contact address. A friend, another relative?

JOSIE. No.

Do you know this probably just shows that this wasn't such a great idea.

She hesitates.

GUARD 2. Are you alright darling?

JOSIE. Yes, I'm fine.

I've been abroad you see.

GUARD 2. Oh, O.K. I understand. (*She doesn't really.*) Do you want to leave things till you're more settled?

JOSIE. Well . . . I think it's now or never to tell you the truth.

Pause.

GUARD 2. Can she write to your work?

JOSIE. I've all that to sort out.

GUARD 2. There must be someone.

JOSIE. No. I haven't got anyone.

GUARD 2. Everyone's got someone.

JOSIE. No.

Pause.

JOSIE. Tell you what . . . I've got a job interview tomorrow, she could send it there?

GUARD 2. I don't know that it'll get to you in time for that.

JOSIE. No but I think I'll get the job. I'm pretty sure.

GUARD 2. But suppose you don't?

JOSIE. I will. And if I don't it's not meant is it?

GUARD 2. That's one way of looking at it.

JOSIE. Let's do that then. Have you got a bit of paper?

GUARD 2 *sorts her out.* JOSIE *takes a pen out of her bag and starts to write quickly.* GUARD 2 *watches her.*

GUARD 2. You look like her.

JOSIE (*startled*). Do I?

GUARD 2. A bit.

I'll tell you something, the nicest people in here are the long termers. Your Mum included, she'd probably be surprised to hear me say that because I can't say we don't have our moments but they're all very well behaved. Nice women . . . calm as cows in a field. I can't work it out really.

JOSIE *finishes writing. She hesitates then hands the note to* GUARD 2.

Now don't worry. I'll make sure she gets it.

JOSIE. Thank you.

GUARD 2. You'll be glad you did that.

FAY*'s room. A very small room. A prison cell.* FAY *is on her hands and knees, cleaning. She dusts under the bed. She rubs at the floor with a cloth. She straightens up, looking round. She checks out her meagre possessions, straightens something, everything is lined up with obsessive neatness. She sits staring into space.* GUARD 1 *stands in the doorway, offering the note.*

FAY. What's that?

GUARD 1. It's from your daughter.

Pause.

FAY. Who?

GUARD 1. Your daughter Josie.

Pause.

FAY. No it's not.

GUARD 1. She's signed it, look. Come on, take it Fay.

Slowly FAY *takes the note, she peers at it suspiciously.*

FAY. What does she want?

GUARD 1. I don't know. I don't read your letters.

FAY. Course you do.

GUARD 1. I think she wants to visit.

FAY. So how would you know that then?

GUARD 1. She came to visit. No visitor's order. We couldn't let her in.

FAY. What? Why not?

GUARD 1. No visitor's order!

FAY. You can't keep her away from me! She's my daughter!

GUARD 1. I'm glad that you want to see her. Of course you want to see her. Just fill in the form.

FAY. Oh I don't know about that . . .

She looks at the note for a moment.

GUARD 1. What does she say?

FAY. I don't know. It's not her handwriting.

GUARD 1. When did she last write to you?

FAY. She's never written to me.

GUARD 1. Maybe her handwriting's changed.

FAY. What do you care!? Nosy bugger.

GUARD 1. I think it'd be good for you to see her. It's only natural.

FAY. I don't know.

She considers the letter a moment.

What does she look like?

GUARD 1. I didn't see her.

FAY. Lovely handwriting.

She strokes the paper as if she can feel the words.

What does she want?

GUARD 1. Read it.

FAY *puts it aside.*

FAY. I'll read it later.

GUARD 1. I'll leave the visitor's request form here shall I?

FAY. What for?

GUARD 1. For you to fill out.

FAY. I don't know how to do that.

GUARD 1. I can help you.

FAY. I don't know.

GUARD 1. Have a think about it.

FAY. Alright.

GUARD 1. You'll be sorry if you don't see her.

FAY. Will I?

Visiting room. It's day. JOSIE *stands at the edge of the visiting room, looking for* FAY. *A great buzz of conversation around them.*

JOSIE *sees* FAY. *She crosses over to her and sits down.*

The GUARDS *stroll through this, there's a concentrated area where* FAY *and* JOSIE *are, outside that, the sense of a great crowd of people talking round them.*

The GUARDS *are not there the whole time, they walk through the scene occasionally, patrolling the waiting room.*

FAY *looks at* JOSIE.

A blank moment.

JOSIE. Hi.

FAY. Oh hullo.

Neither of them speaks for a moment, looking at each other. FAY *quickly grows uncomfortable, looking away, looking round the room.*

You found your way alright then?

JOSIE. Yeah. No problems.

Another pause. JOSIE's *eyes remain fixed on* FAY's *face.* FAY *looks round the room, fidgets nervously.*

FAY. The woman next door nearly killed herself last night.

JOSIE. Did she?

FAY. Yeah. I heard her. She's fractured her skull. I heard her through the wall. Sounded like someone dropping a sack of potatoes. She never made a sound.

JOSIE. Didn't she?

FAY. Not a peep. See what she was doing was falling off the radiator, over and over. She must've got herself up on the radiator and perched there like a seagull. Then she took a dive into the floor. Headfirst. Never put her hands out to break her fall.

JOSIE. That's . . . terrible.

FAY. It is. But you've got to admire her determination eh?
Never put her hands out, headfirst into a stone floor. That's
some death wish. I heard her. (*Imitates noise.*) Boomph! . . .
just like someone throwing down a sack of potatoes. Over
and over. She's fractured her skull.

JOSIE. You knew her?

FAY. Not really. She's been next door two . . . I think it's two
years now but she's an annoying cow. Talks like she's got a
mouthful of mashed potatoes. She wasn't right in the head
before she cracked it open, you know what I mean?

Pause.

Anyway that's her away for a while.

JOSIE. Why did she do it?

FAY. I don't know.

Her kid was up to see her last week. Think it did her head
in.

Actually the easiest way to top yourself round her is to get
in a stone. You can put an edge on anything metal with a
good stone . . . then you can cut . . .

So how're you keeping?

JOSIE. Fine. Good.

FAY. I wouldn't have known you.

JOSIE. No.

Pause.

You look just the same.

FAY. Yeah?

JOSIE. I think so. I recognised you.

FAY. I wouldn't have known you.

JOSIE. Fifteen years.

FAY. As long as that? (*Shakes her head.*)

Pause.

FAY. I don't like what you've done to your hair though.

JOSIE. How do you mean?

FAY. That colour, you should have left it the way it was. More natural. You'd pretty hair.

JOSIE. This is natural.

FAY. Eh?

JOSIE. It . . . maybe it got darker as I got older. This is the colour it is now.

FAY. Oh . . . you should dye it back then.

JOSIE. How long do we get?

FAY. What for?

JOSIE. The visit.

FAY. An hour. I think. It's been a while. An hour it used to be. When I was seeing my solicitor. (*Nerves start to show.*) It said on the paperwork. Did you get all the paperwork? It said on that. Did you get it alright? Did you fill it in alright?

JOSIE. Yes.

FAY. No problems?

JOSIE. No.

FAY. They didn't give you any problems?

JOSIE. No.

FAY. They don't like me some of them. It said everything on that. Length of visit. All that. Did you read it? Is it an hour we've got?

JOSIE. I think so.

FAY. Didn't it say?

JOSIE. I think it's an hour.

FAY. They'll tell us anyway. They won't let us get that wrong. (*Pause*.) I think it's an hour.

The GUARDS *pass strolling up opposite sides of the room, keeping an eye on everything.* FAY *and* JOSIE *watch them pass.*

Pause. FAY *looks for her cigarettes. She's out. In some of the longer pauses the sound of the busy visiting room surges slightly and dies away again.*

FAY. Do you smoke pet?

JOSIE. No. I don't. Thanks.

FAY. No I'm out. You can bring me stuff. Did you see that? You can bring me little things if you put it through the office before you come in. You have to list everything you're bringing in but you can get me cigarettes. You have to write it all down.

JOSIE. I brought you some fruit.

FAY (*disappointed*). Oh.

Pause.

JOSIE. Was that not right?

FAY. No. I'm allowed fruit.

JOSIE. Good . . . good.

Pause. FAY *is still hardly looking at* JOSIE. *Looking round at all the other people.*

FAY. I've not been in here before. Not had a visit in this place before. It's a nice room isn't it? All new paint. Oh they've painted this up nice haven't they? Oh yes. God look at them all. (*Lowering her voice slightly, looking at other prisoners and visitors.*) This is an eye opener this, I'm telling you. This is a day out for me. Seeing them all.

JOSIE. You got a lot of friends then?

FAY. Oh you have a laugh. You know.

Pause.

You think folk are your friends but they're not. That's how it is really.

JOSIE. What do you mean?

FAY *shrugs*.

FAY. I can't eat bananas at all.

JOSIE. Sorry?

FAY. Fruit. I can't stomach bananas. You didn't bring me in any did you?

JOSIE. I don't know. It was like a big . . . It was a fruit basket, you know? I think maybe a couple.

FAY. Another time you could bring me some cigarettes. Or chocolate. Cigarettes and chocolate. That'd be lovely. Get me that . . . If you come again I mean.

JOSIE. I will. If you want me to.

FAY. I don't mind.

Pause.

So, how've you been?

JOSIE. Fine. Good.

FAY. That's a lovely suit. That's a lovely bit of cloth.

JOSIE. Thanks.

FAY. You've done alright for yourself.

JOSIE. I'm in personnel.

FAY. That's good.

Pause.

So what do you do exactly?

JOSIE. People management for a regional chain. I drive around a lot.

JOSIE *shrugs, she's not interested in explaining*.

FAY. Oh . . . Good money?

JOSIE. It's alright. I've been working abroad the last few
years.

FAY. Lovely. Where?

JOSIE. All over. America . . . Europe . . .

FAY. You've seen the sun haven't you? I never get any here.
It's the block opposite you see, Always between me and the
sky unless I lie on the floor, but that'd be daft wouldn't it?

Pause.

Tobacco and papers is best.

JOSIE. Sorry?

FAY. If you're bringing me fags. Makes them go further.

JOSIE. O.K.

Pause.

Have you been here the whole time?

FAY. How do you mean?

JOSIE. The whole . . . I mean have you been here fifteen
years?

FAY. No. Five years here.

JOSIE. Long time.

FAY. It's alright. But there's no proper light, in my room you
know, well I told you that didn't I?

JOSIE. I had a job finding you.

FAY. Did you?

JOSIE. Didn't know where to start.

FAY. There's not that many places to look is there? If they
haven't got you in one place they'll have put you in another.

JOSIE. It was all new to me.

FAY. Well. You found me eh?

JOSIE. Yes.

FAY. You always were clever.

JOSIE *says nothing*.

Still are I expect. What is it? People management?

JOSIE. Yes.

FAY. So what do you do exactly?

JOSIE. It's not that interesting.

FAY. I thought you'd do something artistic. You were always good with your hands.

JOSIE. Was I?

FAY. Ever so clever. So have you got a boyfriend?

JOSIE. I'm divorced.

FAY. Are you?

JOSIE. Yes.

FAY (*faint, shocked*). Fancy that.

Pause.

Didn't he treat you right?

JOSIE. We just didn't get on. We were too young I think.

FAY. That would do it.

Pause.

No boyfriend then.

JOSIE. No.

Pause.

Listen . . . you must be wondering . . . you must have wondered why I never came before.

FAY. Oh no. You're alright. We don't need to talk about that. Did you come in a car then, have you got a car?

JOSIE. Yes . . . You see Mum . . . Gran wouldn't ever talk about it so I . . .

FAY (*interrupts*). How is the old fag butt?

JOSIE (*thrown*). Well . . . she died.

FAY. Eh?

JOSIE. Didn't you know?

FAY. No. No why would they tell me that? She was his mother . . . Jesus.

JOSIE. It was cancer. She just had a bit of a cough . . . a year last May this was. I was nagging her to go in but when she did they said there was nothing . . .

FAY (*interrupts*). Are you keeping an eye on the clock here? We've been talking an awful long time.

JOSIE. It's only . . .

FAY. Ages.

JOSIE. We're fine.

FAY. Oh . . . Good.

Pause.

JOSIE (*looking round*). This isn't too bad is it?

FAY. What isn't?

JOSIE. This place.

FAY. You think so do you?

JOSIE. Well, I mean . . . there's flowers out there.

FAY. Eh?

JOSIE. Acres of them. Trees. Grass.

FAY. And do you see me skipping across it with a picnic basket? Oh they make it look good.

JOSIE. No it's just not what I expected.

FAY. What did you expect?

JOSIE. Barbed wire, Rottweilers. I didn't expect geraniums.

Pause.

FAY. It's not what you think. It's not a hotel.

JOSIE. I was joking. I'm sorry.

FAY. It's no joke.

JOSIE. Just more cheerful than I thought.

FAY (*upset*). Well. There you go.

JOSIE. Well . . . that's good isn't it?

FAY. What?

JOSIE. That you're not all locked up in iron bars and concrete.

FAY. I could see how you'd think that.

> *Pause.*

> This is a long time to sit without a fag. What time is it?

> JOSIE *shows her watch.* FAY *reaches out to it.*

> Oh that's beautiful. Haven't you got beautiful things?

JOSIE (*still offering it*). Here. Try it on.

> FAY *looks at the* GUARDS, *shaking her head.*

FAY. We're not allowed to touch.

> JOSIE *looks at* GUARD 2. GUARD 2 *is watching them.*
> *She smiles.*

JOSIE. They won't mind. I've talked to that one. She's O.K.

FAY. She's a cow. We're not allowed.

JOSIE. Really?

FAY (*leaning back, hands ostentatiously held up and empty*).
Stop it. You'll get me into trouble.

> JOSIE *leans back.*

JOSIE. I'm not doing this very well am I?

FAY. Doing what?

JOSIE. I just don't know how to get into it.

FAY. Oh you don't want to get into anything. So. Your Gran's dead?

JOSIE. Yes.

FAY. Was she bad, at the end?

JOSIE. She wasn't herself.

FAY. She used to love me. She said I was the daughter she never had. Suppose that was you in the end . . .

A pause. FAY is trembling.

She never visited me. She never came near me. I don't know what she told you . . . What she must have told you about me . . . and your Dad . . . Oh this is no good, this is no good . . . (*She's shaking, on the verge of tears.*) Look I'm getting all upset. I want to go back. I want to go back to my room. I want to go.

FAY starts to get up.

JOSIE. Shhhh, no, don't please, don't go . . .

FAY. You don't know what you've done! You don't! I'm all over the place now. I could . . . I've seen women piss themselves coming in for visits, just . . . Is that what you want to do to me? You want to see me sitting here greiting in a puddle like a great baby. Do you!?

JOSIE. Have you wet yourself?

FAY. What do you think I am?

She looks round checking out the GUARDS.

They're looking now. They'll take me back. I should go back.

JOSIE. Please just sit down. Please.

Reluctantly FAY sits again. She takes a few deep breaths, getting herself under control.

FAY. Look. This isn't how you do things. You need to learn how to behave . . .

JOSIE. I'm sorry.

FAY. It's not the zoo you know, you can't come in when the fancy takes you and throw me a bun! Fuck's sake! Give me a bit of small talk at least tell me about the weather or . . . Christ I canny take this in . . .

Pause. JOSIE *sits, tense.* FAY *won't look at her.*

JOSIE. I'm sorry. Maybe we'll do this another time.

FAY *instantly changes.*

FAY. Oh no oh don't, no don't, don't go. I haven't seen you in such a long . . . such a long time. (*Starts to cry.*) My wee girl. My wee girl . . .

JOSIE *watches as* FAY *snuffles, groping in her sleeve for a hanky she hasn't got. She wipes her face with her hands.*

JOSIE. It's sunny. The weather's warm.

FAY. I can see that.

JOSIE. I shouldn't have upset you.

FAY. It's fine. I'm fine.

JOSIE. I wanted to ask you . . .

FAY. No! Just wait will you.

I don't like to get upset. There's nowhere to go with it.

JOSIE. No.

FAY. I need to settle myself. This is no good. No good at all. Tell me something.

JOSIE. What?

FAY. What did you have for breakfast?

JOSIE. Sorry?

FAY. Tell me. Please. Just keep talking to me.

JOSIE. Toast.

FAY. Hot?

JOSIE. Aye.

FAY. Butter?

JOSIE. Olive spread.

FAY. What's that?

JOSIE. It's an olive oil spread.

FAY. Is it like butter?

JOSIE. It's better for you.

FAY. Is that like a slimming thing?

JOSIE. I suppose.

FAY (*quickly, before she can panic again*). Tell me something else.

JOSIE. Did Dad brush his teeth in the kitchen sink?

FAY. What?

JOSIE. I've got a very clear memory of that, Dad brushing his teeth in the kitchen sink when it was still full of dirty pans and plates. And you shouted at him, and he looked at you with his mouth full of foam. And he looked like a dog you'd caught with its nose in a biscuit tin.

FAY. That's dirty.

JOSIE. Did he do that? Is that the sort of thing he'd do?

FAY. How would I know now?

Pause.

JOSIE. Mum never talked about him. It made her cry.

FAY. Your Gran?

JOSIE. Yes.

FAY. You called her Mum?

JOSIE. . . . Yes.

FAY. That would've killed me if I'd thought about it.

JOSIE. I'm . . . sorry.

FAY. It's alright. She's dead now.

JOSIE. Yes.

FAY. Can't speak ill of the dead.

Pause.

Your Dad would have been glad to see how you turned out.

JOSIE. Would he?

FAY. Tell the truth he'd've rather you were a rock star. He
wanted to be a rock star. Bugger was tone deaf but he loved
his guitar. Punk. Punk was his big chance. Tone deaf was an
asset for punk wasn't it?

JOSIE. I don't know really.

FAY. Course you don't. You don't remember back then. What
am I thinking of?

JOSIE. What . . . ? (*Suddenly she can't speak.*)

FAY. Yes?

JOSIE *shakes her head.*

Go on. You were going to ask me something?

JOSIE. What did he look like?

FAY. Your Dad? Oh he was a looker. I thought he was a looker,
had a bit of a gut on him but he was gorgeous. Didn't your
Gran have photos?

JOSIE. Yes . . . but only when he was younger . . . before . . .

FAY. You're upset aren't you? Don't go getting upset. It's
alright.

JOSIE. Is it O.K? Are you O.K? You don't mind talking about
him?

FAY. No. I don't mind. Did you think I would?

JOSIE. You just said . . . I don't want to upset you again.

FAY. I often think about your Dad.

JOSIE. Do you?

FAY. I miss him. I miss him yet.

JOSIE (*quiet*). Do you?

FAY. Yes. (*Looking at* JOSIE.) Oh now I know you. Now I can see you. You look about ten years old. Don't sweetie. Don't upset yourself.

JOSIE. I'm fine.

FAY. Course you are.

JOSIE. I'm fine. Really.

FAY. I remember every moment of your life from when you were born till the day they took me away from you. I remember what you looked like, what you wore, how your hair was, what you said . . . what you felt.

JOSIE. Have you got photographs?

FAY. No. I haven't got anything.

JOSIE. Wouldn't they let you bring them?

FAY. She wouldn't let me. She kept everything.

JOSIE. I never saw them.

FAY. She probably burnt them. She probably hated me.

Pause.

Didn't she?

JOSIE. I don't know.

FAY. She was his mother.

We used to go out every Friday night. Just her and me.

JOSIE. What did you do?

FAY. We'd have three drinks in the White Rose then we'd have an Italian at Donatello's . . . I loved Donatello's, is it still there? Corner of the High Street?

JOSIE. I don't know. We moved.

FAY. Course you did. I couldn't find you. I didn't know where you were.

JOSIE. You looked for me?

FAY. I asked. They wouldn't tell me where you were.

JOSIE. But that's . . . they shouldn't do that should they?

FAY. It doesn't matter. You found me.

JOSIE. That's terrible . . .

FAY. Oh that's the least of it.

JOSIE. But we should complain!

FAY. I don't like thinking about it. I don't like upsetting myself.
    I'd rather remember the good times, Donatello's and your
    Nan all done up with green eyeshadow and you still sitting
    up when I got in, asleep on your Dad's lap in front of the
    fire.

    JOSIE *catches her breath*.

    Remember?

JOSIE. No . . . I . . .

FAY. Tell me about yourself.

JOSIE. I don't know . . .

FAY. You're pretty. You've got lovely clothes, a bit of money.
    You've had your heart broken once at least . . .

JOSIE. Not really I . . .

FAY. Well you're divorced, whatever . . . no steady love now,
    jetting round the world . . .

JOSIE. No.

FAY. No? You're better than television. I haven't experienced
    anything past the eight o'clock watershed for fifteen years.
    No sex, no drugs, no rock and roll . . . I'm getting light
    headed just looking at you. How's your social life? What
    clubs do you go to? What's the last place you had a drink
    that wasn't in Britain?

JOSIE. San Diego.

FAY. There you go. Where's that then?

JOSIE. California.

FAY. California. With the oranges and the sunshine. What did you have?

JOSIE. God . . . I can't remember that.

FAY. Try. Go on. Tell me.

JOSIE. I don't know . . . a beer? Maybe a margherita.

FAY. That sounds like the business. That's with tequila?

JOSIE. Yes.

FAY. That's a mad drink, tequila.

JOSIE. Yes.

FAY (*laughing*). Isn't it? What was the place like? What's San Diego like?

JOSIE. It's . . . It's a huge city. Glass and metal skyscrapers and it's got a zoo . . .

FAY. Oh lovely. Lions and tigers and bears?

JOSIE (*uncertain*). Eh . . . yeah. And it's got a beach . . . Well it's got about eighty beaches, right in the city. People walk out their houses and onto a surf board.

FAY. California eh? And where were you? Was it a nice hotel?

JOSIE. It was alright.

FAY. Were you on expenses?

JOSIE. Yes.

FAY. God, what's that like? Do you empty the mini bar?

JOSIE. You keep your receipts.

FAY. So you were drinking a margherita . . .

JOSIE. Yes.

FAY. What was the bar like? Who were you with?

JOSIE. It was . . . I was in the old town. That's up on the hill. It's . . . well it's not really old.

FAY. How d'you mean?

JOSIE. It's American old. Anything older than me is an antique you know?

FAY. God you've really been to America haven't you? Tell me.

JOSIE. It's nice.

FAY. Come on darlin', let me see it. What did it look like?

JOSIE. I don't know what you . . . ?

FAY (*interrupts*). Give me a picture. What did you see?

JOSIE (*hesitates*). Little low houses with red and orange walls and roofs, there's trolley buses, that's trams . . . and a view over the bay . . . The air smells of charcoal and barbecue and bushes with flowers the size of hats grow like weeds.

FAY. Aw lovely . . .

JOSIE. . . . And I was sitting outside this bar, under a palm roof, watching a mariachi band annoy the tourists at the restaurant next door . . .

FAY. What's that?

JOSIE. Guys in Mexican hats with trumpets.

FAY. Right. I knew that.

JOSIE. So I was just, drinking my drink there. With Dave.

FAY. Ah here we go. Who's Dave?

JOSIE. He works in the San Diego office of the company I was with.

FAY. Nice?

JOSIE. Gorgeous. Gay.

FAY. Aw bad luck. What did you do? What did you talk about?

JOSIE. This and that. We watched the sunset.

FAY. Lovely.

JOSIE. Watched all the skateboarders going past . . .

FAY. See now I've got a picture of you. Now I'm getting an idea who you are. It's like a postcard.

JOSIE. Dave said to me he was a demon on a skateboard when he was nine or ten but when he grew older he worried too much about injuring himself to enjoy it. And he asked me if I'd felt the same way about my bike. Did I have a bicycle when I was little? When did I stop riding it . . .

FAY. You never had a bike though, you said you wanted a puppy instead.

JOSIE. And I said to him I couldn't remember. I didn't know if I'd had a bicycle or not.

FAY. No. You wanted a puppy but it would've been too much mess love. We got you a hamster and a trip to Butlin's at Prestwick. You loved that, splashing about in the pool. Remember?

JOSIE. No. I don't. I don't remember a thing before my eleventh birthday. Not a sight not a sound not a smell . . . nothing. I look back and my head's empty as a balloon.

FAY. That's sad.

JOSIE. And I told Dave this . . . I'd never told anyone. Never really realised that was what was going on . . . And he said that was terrible, that was like living in a house built on mud . . . you never knew when it would rise up through the floorboards and swallow you up.

FAY. This Dave's got some imagination.

JOSIE. And I thought . . . that's exactly what it feels like. And about a week later I quit that job. And I came home.

FAY. But you've got yourself another job?

JOSIE. Oh yes.

FAY. Good. I don't want you worrying about money.

Pause.

JOSIE. So that's it. That's why I came to see you.

FAY. Why's that?

JOSIE. I've got no memories, but you have. You know everything.

Pause.

FAY. Oh.

I didn't know I had anything no-one else could get. And you want to take that?

JOSIE. I just wanted to talk to you.

Pause.

FAY. Well . . . you're my Josie after all. I suppose you're entitled.

JOSIE. Nothing you don't want to talk about just . . . ordinary things.

FAY. Like what?

JOSIE. Anything.

FAY (*laughing*). Where the dustbins were? What colour were the tea towels? Did you like fish fingers?

JOSIE. Yes! . . . Anything.

Pause.

FAY. Round the side of the house.

JOSIE. What?

FAY. The dustbins. There was a passage down the side of the house. Had a hedge on one side? The bins were just before the kitchen door.

JOSIE. Was the wall white? The side wall of the house?

FAY. Yeah.

JOSIE. I think . . .

FAY. You remember it?

JOSIE. I don't know. Were there snails under the hedge?

FAY. You remember it. What colour was the back door?

JOSIE *thinks*.

JOSIE. Blue? With a glass panel at the top.

FAY. There you go. Now you open the back door and the cooker's in front of you and I've got the tea towels hanging over the handle of the grill. You can't tell me what colour they are because you must've seen a hundred tea towels come and go but what colour's the wall above the cooker?

Pause.

JOSIE. Green?

FAY. No . . .

JOSIE. Yellow!

FAY. That's it. And I've got fish fingers under the grill. Do you want to eat them?

JOSIE. No.

FAY. No. You'll hide them under your beans won't you and bash them about till their orange coats come off and even a dog wouldn't eat them.

JOSIE. Yes.

FAY. See? You remember.

JOSIE *bursts into tears.*

FAY. Don't get upset. Don't get upset. Our time's nearly up now. It's alright. You're O.K.

JOSIE (*getting herself together*). Yes.

FAY. You're alright. Don't let them see. Don't.

JOSIE (*snuffling*). Who?

FAY *jerks her head at the* GUARDS. *They are looking.*

JOSIE. I'm sorry. I'm O.K . . .

FAY. I know you are. It's upsetting all this isn't it? We're both upset. Only natural.

JOSIE. Yes.

FAY. Are you going to come and see me again?

JOSIE. I . . . if you want me to?

FAY. You want to, don't you?

Pause.

JOSIE. Yes.

FAY. It's only natural, isn't it? Like salmon. Swimming upstream. Sooner or later you have to go back to where you came from. It's natural.

JOSIE. Yes.

FAY. There's something I need to ask you though. You were married, yes?

JOSIE. Divorced now . . .

FAY. Yes but you were. And were you in love?

JOSIE (*hesitates*). I . . .

FAY. Were you really in love or did you just think you were?

JOSIE. I've been in love.

FAY. Just not with him?

JOSIE *won't answer.*

FAY. That's O.K. You don't need to tell me that. I just need to know that you realise what it's like . . . to be in love.

JOSIE. I do.

FAY. Good. Then we'll be able to understand each other.

JOSIE. You're talking about my Dad aren't you?

FAY. As long as you can understand me. Do you think you can?

Pause.

JOSIE. I'll try.

FAY. That's great darlin'. And I'll try and remember everything for you.

GUARDS 1 *and* 2 *start clapping their hands and calling out. The sound of the crowd in the visiting room surges up again.*

GUARD 1. Time!

GUARD 2. That's time now ladies and gentlemen please!

FAY. Will you come again?

JOSIE. Yes. Of course.

FAY *gets up. She looks back at* JOSIE.

FAY. Your Dad kept the garden beautiful. Like a pensioner. All groomed and pruned and full of roses . . . What colour were the roses Josie?

Pause while JOSIE *struggles to think.*

JOSIE. Pink?

FAY *smiles.*

FAY. There you go now.

JOSIE *and* GUARD 1 *exit.* FAY *and* GUARD 2 *move to the prison garden.*

The prison garden. FAY *has gardening materials. She starts planting out seedlings.* GUARD 2 *watches.*

GUARD 2 *notices something on her skirt. She brushes at it, irritated.* FAY *looks at her.*

GUARD 2. I think it's yoghurt. Baby porridge, whatever she was chucking out of her high chair this morning.

FAY (*laughs*). Oh God they all do it don't they?

GUARD 2 *offers* FAY *a cigarette.*

FAY *is surprised. This is not normal at the moment. She takes one, pleased but wary.*

Thanks.

GUARD 2. Don't look so surprised. I can still have a Mrs Smiley day now and then can't I?

She lights FAY's *cigarette.* FAY *starts to go on working.*

Och leave that a while. Enjoy your fag.

FAY *glances at her warily then obeys. Sitting more comfortably, drawing on her cigarette.*

So that was your daughter you had in the other day?

FAY (*wary*). Yes.

GUARD 2. You won't have seen her in a while eh?

FAY. No.

GUARD 2. How long?

FAY (*hesitates*). Fifteen years.

GUARD 2. All the time you've been in?

FAY. Yes.

GUARD 2. You haven't seen her all the time you've been in?

FAY. They wouldn't tell me where she was.

GUARD 2. But you could've asked. They have to give you the information if you ask or you get your solicitor to ask.

FAY. They wouldn't tell me. I asked, the night I came in.

GUARD 2. The night you came in?

FAY. You know what it's like. Everyone was talking at me.

GUARD 2. You've not asked since then?

FAY. Tearing the clothes off me, sticking me in the shower. I'm screaming at everyone 'Where's Josie? Where's my wee . . . ' (*Chokes back distress.*)

GUARD 2. Fifteen years and you never asked again?

FAY. I'm screaming 'Josie! I have to get home for Josie!' Bashed my head off the shower tiles. First morning in prison I was in the Infirmary.

GUARD 2. You could've asked anytime. Written to her . . . Couldn't you?

FAY *says nothing.*

Couldn't you Fay?

FAY. They wouldn't tell me where she was. She had her own life.

GUARD 2. You could've written to her. Plenty do. Don't they?

FAY. I was screaming for her. The pain nearly killed me.

GUARD 2. Is that right? You never talked to me about her and we talked a lot, didn't we Fay? Well. So. You've seen her now. Did it feel like seeing your daughter?

FAY. I hardly knew her.

GUARD 2. She'll have grown a bit eh? How old was she when you murdered her Dad?

FAY. I didn't . . . You don't know what I did.

GUARD 2. Course I do Fay I read your case file four years ago and I remember it fine. Oh everyone's innocent in here.

FAY *stubs out the rest of her cigarette without comment, throwing the butt away.*

GUARD 2. Don't you want to save that for later?

FAY *ignores her, starts gardening again.*

GUARD 2. I bet you'll want that later.

So she'll have been a wee girl then, what was she, nine? Ten? Does it still feel like you have a daughter or is it like some woman coming to see you out of nowhere? Why did she come now anyway?

FAY. I don't know.

GUARD 2. I'm only asking because of my wee girl. I'm trying to imagine it. You can understand that. It's only natural.

FAY. I don't know about that.

GUARD 2. You're a warning to us all Fay. Why didn't you just leave him? Take the little one and leave him? Why did you kill him? Your little girl's Dad? What did he do to you? What were you thinking?

FAY *says nothing.*

I'd love to know what was in your head. I can't make sense of it at all.

FAY. Don't think about it then.

GUARD 2. Don't be cheeky Fay. So is she coming to visit you today?

FAY. I don't know.

GUARD 2. Didn't you send her a visitor's order?

FAY. You know I did.

GUARD 2. But you don't know whether she's coming or not?

FAY. No.

GUARD 2. She hasn't phoned?

FAY. No.

GUARD 2. Well you'll know soon won't you? Five minutes to visiting time. I'll either be taking you down to the visitors room or back to your room won't I? You'll know any minute.

FAY. Yes.

GUARD 2. You're not that bothered are you?

FAY *says nothing. She starts to clear up the gardening equipment.*

GUARD 2. You could be my Mum couldn't you? Can't get my head round it at all. You're ages with my Mum aren't you? That poor woman. What did she want to see you about anyway, after all this time?

FAY. I don't know.

GUARD 2. Curious maybe? Wants to know where she came from.

FAY. I don't know.

GUARD 2. God. I wouldn't. Are you done there?

FAY. Yes.

GUARD 2 *starts to walk* FAY *back to the visiting room.
She stops her, does a quick pat down search.*

GUARD 2. So what do you think Fay? Visitors' room or back
to your room?

FAY *just stands, showing nothing.*

You don't care do you? Visitors' room. Come on.

GUARD 1 *is waiting outside the visiting room.* GUARD 2
walks FAY *towards him.*

Bet you don't even like gardening. None of you do. It's the
fresh air you like isn't it? The change of view. Weeding's a
privilege. I think they should make ironing a privilege. I
could bring in loads.

JOSIE *walks into the visiting room and sits, waiting.*

GUARD 1. Ironing? I could tell you about ironing.

GUARD 2. No you couldn't George.

GUARD 1. Shirts and cuffs. That's the crucial part.

GUARD 2. You don't know you're born Fay. One room to
clean and no-one else to mess it up. You should have my
house to clean after a ten-hour shift.

FAY. I like gardening. I had a garden. We had petunias and
bulbs and raspberry bushes. I had tomatoes by the kitchen
door. I had the only kept garden on the road.

GUARD 2. Course you did Fay.

GUARD 2 *exits,* GUARD 1 *looks at his list.*

GUARD 1. Your daughter's in again Fay. That's nice isn't it?

FAY. Yes.

GUARD 1. Off you go then.

FAY *walks into the visitors' room and sits down opposite
JOSIE again. The sound of the visitors surges up again.*

FAY. Hullo.

JOSIE. Hullo.

FAY. I wasn't sure if you would come back.

JOSIE. But I said I would!

FAY. I wasn't sure you'd want to, when you had time to think about it.

JOSIE. I promised.

FAY. Well . . . everyone's always very certain when they make a promise aren't they? But then you have to live the life you promised. Then you know.

JOSIE. I suppose . . .

FAY. I mean there's you divorced . . . I promise I'll stay with him, in sickness and in health till death do us part . . . How many years did you do in the end?

Pause. This is upsetting JOSIE.

JOSIE. I . . . six months or so but . . .

FAY (*interrupts*). And you were on the rebound.

JOSIE. . . . I never said that.

FAY. Och darlin'. You didn't need to. Was he married?

JOSIE. Who?

FAY. The one you really loved.

JOSIE *says nothing,* FAY *takes it as confirmation.*

So you thought 'Look I'll be married too, how do you like that?'

JOSIE. I . . . I didn't think that was what I was doing.

FAY. There's no-one can hurt you like the one you love, is there? Drives us all to madness. It's ourselves we hurt in the end isn't it?

JOSIE *says nothing for a moment.*

JOSIE. Everyone's looking at you.

FAY. They're not used to seeing me out. I've never had a visitor before last week.

Pause.

They look 'cause I'm rarer than a unicorn, there's only about half a dozen of us in the whole country.

JOSIE. Half a dozen what?

FAY. Women who've killed someone.

Pause.

JOSIE. I thought . . . (*She suddenly can't go on.*)

FAY. What?

JOSIE *shakes her head. She can't speak.*

FAY. No, go on.

JOSIE (*quiet*). I thought you always said you hadn't? I mean you didn't plead guilty.

FAY. Do you believe me?

JOSIE *doesn't know what to say.*

It's what I'm sentenced for.

JOSIE. Yes . . .

FAY. What did your Gran say?

JOSIE. She said . . .

FAY. Yes?

JOSIE. Once she said if she hadn't been able to see Dad's face in mine she'd've thrown me in the river to drown.

Pause.

FAY. That sounds like her.

Pause.

This man you loved, do you ever see him now?

JOSIE. I don't want to talk about that.

FAY. Don't you?

JOSIE. No.

FAY. Well . . . I nearly didn't fill in the form for your visitor's pass. I nearly changed my mind.

JOSIE. But . . . We agreed! You wanted me to come back!

FAY. I nearly changed my mind. It's a very painful thing, remembering and you're asking me to do it for both of us.

Pause.

I bet you think you'll never fall in love again?

JOSIE *says nothing.*

There you go. I couldn't get past your Dad now, even remembering the worst of it.

JOSIE. What was the worst of it?

FAY. Never mind.

Some of the fighting was terrible. It still upsets me remembering that. He knew how to hurt me.

Can you do something for me? Can let your hair down for me? Now hold it back at the sides.

JOSIE *hesitates then obeys.*

Now shake it out?

JOSIE *does so.*

Now that's nice. That suits you. We do hairdressing lessons in here you know. We've got a choice, hairdressing, sewing or cleaning. Very forward thinking isn't it? Very 21st century. We'll be ready for the world when we get out won't we? We'll be able to trim a fringe, sweep up the bits and stuff a cushion with them.

JOSIE. When do you get out?

Pause.

FAY. You really don't know anything do you? I don't sweetheart. Not until they reckon I'm no longer a danger to society. And I'm as much of a danger as I ever was. Ain't I?

JOSIE. How do you mean?

FAY. I'm the same person as I was when they locked me up. If they think that's bad I suppose they'll just have to keep me here. I haven't changed. What happened to my things?

JOSIE. What?

FAY. My ornaments, my clothes, my jewellery. Did she take them? Did she sell them?

JOSIE. I don't know.

FAY. How much did she leave? Some of that must be mine. We should work it out sometime. I could use a bit of extra cash.

JOSIE. You need money?

FAY. Well you know, a chocolate biscuit is an adventure if you can't afford one.

JOSIE. I can give you money.

FAY. No no. You're alright. I only want what's mine. We'll find some way of working it out.

JOSIE. She didn't leave much but . . .

FAY. We don't need to worry about that just now. How's the new job?

JOSIE. Oh it's fine. Settling into it.

FAY. My God. There's you making dirt pies with jam round your face and here's you walking into jobs. Meeting new people. You love that don't you?

Pause.

JOSIE. I've been travelling around a lot . . .

FAY. But you've got a lot of friends.

JOSIE. Not really. Who was I friendly with then?

FAY (*interrupts*). What about this Dave? In America?

JOSIE. He's in America.

GUARD 2 *is walking slowly past them at this point. not apparently listening.*

FAY. Well aren't you writing to him?

JOSIE. I sent him an e.mail.

FAY. Oh it's all computers now isn't it? I've never seen one. Only on the telly. Can you believe it? If they ever let me out I'd be wandering around like a dodo.

GUARD 2 *is right on top of them.*

GUARD 2. Kate.

FAY. Excuse me this is a private conversation.

GUARD 2. Kate. In Room 45. The next door room to you. She's doing an Open University course in criminal psychology on a personal computer. Plus there's a few in the office that might have caught your eye over the last five years.

FAY. Isn't this a private conversation?

GUARD 2. Just helping you out.

GUARD 2 *wanders off again.*

FAY. Cow. Fucking cow. Excuse me. I've never used one. That's what I meant.

JOSIE. I know.

FAY. Calling me a liar. I've seen them but I wouldn't know how to use one. That's what I was saying.

JOSIE. Yes. I understand.

FAY. Like she knows what I mean. Like she knows what's in my head. You see? You see what I was telling you? They just want to cut you down.

FAY *is glowering after* GUARD 2. JOSIE *is embarrassed.*

You know what she wants? She wants to make me angry. She wants you to see me angry so you won't trust me anymore. Everyone's going to snap sooner or later aren't they? If you push them hard enough.

JOSIE. What do you do?

FAY. Oh I'm terrible. I take rooms apart with my teeth. But I can't help myself, I can't, they drive me to it. You can see that can't you?

Pause.

JOSIE. Once . . . this man I was seeing . . .

FAY. The one you were crazy about? The married one?

JOSIE. Yes. He could be really annoying you know? He'd say, 'Well you're always upset about something aren't you darling? I don't think I can take a day off work for a conversation every time you're upset can I?' And then he'd leave. So this day, he left . . . and I burnt all his suits.

FAY. You didn't.

JOSIE. They were made to measure. He loved his suits. It was quite a bonfire. The neighbours complained about smoke drifting over their washing.

FAY. Did it feel great?

JOSIE. For a while . . . But it put me in the wrong. Not him.

FAY (*laughing*). You see it's in your blood. It's in your blood. We'll never be anyone's doormat, you and me.

JOSIE. Did you do things like that?

FAY. Oh all the time!

JOSIE. To Dad?

FAY (*laughing*). God no! He'd've taken the back of his hand to me!

JOSIE. He hit you?

FAY *doesn't answer straight away, considering.*

FAY. I loved your Dad. That's why he upset me so much. Well you know what it's like don't you?

JOSIE. Yes.

FAY. It's the same for anyone. Anyone that has feelings. If you're a living person, a feeling person, sooner or later you'll lose control of your feelings won't you? If you're alive at all!

JOSIE. Yes.

FAY. Just never lose it with a kitchen knife in your hand. That's my advice to you.

They're both shocked, FAY *tries to keep herself under control then visibly starts to crumble.*

(*quietly*). Oh there you are . . . Oh that's all I can do now darling. That's all I can tell you.

FAY *is shaking.* JOSIE *doesn't know what to do.*

JOSIE. Are you alright?

FAY. Oh God I don't know. Oh help me.

JOSIE. It's O.K. You're O.K.

JOSIE *reaches over and holds onto* FAY. *The* GUARDS *see and exchange a look.* GUARD 1 *starts to move over.*

FAY. Oh help me. I can't.

JOSIE. It's O.K.

GUARD 1. Sorry love. No touching.

JOSIE. What?

GUARD 1. Let her go now.

FAY *is even more upset.*

FAY. Leave us alone! Why can't you leave us alone!

JOSIE. She's upset!

GUARD 1 *tries to gently disengage* JOSIE.

GUARD 1. No touching. That's the rule.

FAY *is clinging on to* JOSIE.

FAY. Leave her! You can't take her away again. Not again!

GUARD 2 *moves over to help.*

JOSIE. Stop it! Don't!

GUARD 2. Alright Fay. Cut it out or the visit's over. I'm warning you!

FAY. She's my daughter! You can't take her from me!

GUARD 1. Calm down Fay.

GUARD 2. This visit is over.

FAY. No!

GUARD 2. Cut it out Fay!

GUARD 1 *and 2 have succeeded in detaching* FAY, *they restrain her while* JOSIE *watches.*

FAY. You can't stop the visit. We've ten minutes left.

GUARD 2. Well are you going to behave yourself madam? Do you think you can remember how to behave in public?

JOSIE. Don't talk to her like that.

GUARD 2. Sweetheart. You don't know her. I do.

JOSIE. Of course I know her. She's my mother.

GUARD 2 *stares at* JOSIE *for a moment then she snorts.*

GUARD 2. And you'll have to be searched before you go. You both will.

GUARD 2 *moves away.* GUARD 1 *is still holding* FAY, *soothing her as much as restraining her.*

GUARD 1. Are you going to be alright now?

FAY. I'm fine. Let go of me.

GUARD 1 *lets her go. He moves away. Both* GUARDS *keep a close eye on* JOSIE *and* FAY *for the rest of the scene.*

FAY (*quiet, upset*). I'm sorry. I'm sorry you had to see that darling. I'm sorry.

JOSIE. It's O.K.

FAY. Oh God, look at them watching me! Everyone's watching me, I can't bear it.

JOSIE (*glaring at* GUARDS). Can't you back off a little?

> GUARD 1 *moves a little further away.* GUARD 2 *holds her ground, arms folded, glowering back.*

FAY. You see? You see what it's like? They want me to fall apart.

JOSIE. Just ignore them.

FAY. They do it all the time. They do it when I'm coming up for review of sentence. Just so it's there on my records, the ink still wet on the writing. Insubordinate behaviour. Erratic impulse control.

JOSIE. Don't let them get to you.

FAY. Sweetheart. My baby. After fifteen years they own me. I'm a piece of play dough for them.

JOSIE. You're better than that.

FAY. How do you know?

JOSIE. I know what I see.

FAY. You know I'm your mother when you look at me?

JOSIE. Yes.

FAY. Oh I don't know if I can bear that.

> JOSIE *waits for her to get herself under control, she half reaches out to her, glances at the* GUARDS *then draws her hand back.*

> The only reason you can look at me at all is because you can't remember your Dad. If you could see him . . .

JOSIE. I can't. I can't.

FAY. Oh God I loved him so. He made me laugh when I was in labour. It doesn't get better than that does it?

JOSIE. I don't know.

FAY. You'd sit beside him when he was digging the garden. Your feet bare so you didn't get your white socks dirty in the earth and he'd dig and you'd point at a worm and go

'Worm,' and he'd say 'That's right Josie that's a worm.'
And you'd see another one. 'Worm,' 'That's right Josie,'
he'd say again, 'That's a worm . . . ' And he could dig that
garden all afternoon and you'd never get tired of watching
the worms and he'd never get tired of watching them with
you. Do you remember that?

JOSIE. I remember a garden. I remember this woman, really
pretty in a pink dress. She lifted my bare legs clear of the
nettles. Who would that be?

FAY. That was me darling.

Will you do me a favour Josie?

JOSIE. What?

FAY. Will you have a night out? Make some friends?

JOSIE. What do you mean?

FAY. Just . . . go out. Drinking or . . . dancing. I don't know. I
know what I would have done at your age . . . Well I had
you younger than your age but I still kicked my heels up!

JOSIE. I wouldn't know where to go.

FAY. Oh try Josie. For me. You loved dancing. You were such
a bright little thing. I can't stand to see you so serious.

JOSIE. Am I?

FAY. So lonely.

JOSIE. I'm not . . .

FAY *interrupts.*

FAY. Wear a red dress. You suit red.

JOSIE. I don't have a red dress.

FAY. Well you can buy one. You're working aren't you?

The GUARDS *move up and down the room, calling time.*

GUARD 1. That's time!

GUARD 2. Wind it up please! Time!

FAY *gets up.*

FAY (*urgent*). Promise me Josie. One night. For me.

JOSIE. Alright.

FAY. That's my girl.

GUARD 2 *is standing over* JOSIE.

GUARD 2. I'll have to ask you to come with me for a body search Miss Kerr. Fay, you know the score, search then lock down. Off you go.

FAY *smiles at* JOSIE *as she moves off. Ignoring* GUARD 2.

FAY. And take your hair down, yes?

FAY *moves away.*

GUARD 2. This way please Miss Kerr.

GUARD 2 *leads* JOSIE *to an area off the visiting room.*

Could you show me your bag please Miss Kerr?

JOSIE *hands it to her, watches as she searches it.*

JOSIE. She was upset. She wanted me to hold her.

GUARD 2 (*ignoring this*). That's fine. Could you take your coat off for me now please Miss Kerr?

JOSIE *does so, hands it over.*

JOSIE. What are you looking for?

GUARD 2. Anything Fay may have passed to you.

JOSIE. It's more likely I'd pass her something isn't it?

GUARD 2. That's why she's being searched too.

JOSIE (*grins*). A nailfile in a cake.

GUARD 2. You've never visited a prison before have you Miss Kerr? Arms up please.

JOSIE *raises her arms.* GUARD 2 *pats her down.*

JOSIE. No.

GUARD 2. No. It shows.

JOSIE. What's that supposed to mean?

GUARD 2 is quickly patting her down.

GUARD 2. It's nothing to do with me. But I tell you this. You won't even see her coming. I didn't.

I need to check your hair.

JOSIE. Jesus.

She stands and lets GUARD 2 run her hands through her hair.

You're right. It's nothing to do with you.

GUARD 2 stops her search.

GUARD 2. She's got you already hasn't she? She's wriggled her way in.

JOSIE. She's my mother.

GUARD 2. And you've visited her twice and now you know she's innocent.

JOSIE. That's not important . . . I don't want to talk about this with you.

GUARD 2. I knew her a long time and she still got me. Tugged all the sympathy out of me. It's a trick. It's something she knows how to do.

JOSIE. And you think she should stay in here forever?

GUARD 2. If anyone should.

JOSIE. Well . . . I'm sure you're entitled to your opinion. Helps you do the job I expect.

GUARD 2. Aw God help you. Mouth.

JOSIE. Excuse me?

GUARD 2 *(taking out torch).* I need to check your mouth.

JOSIE hesitates in embarrassment and disbelief then gapes her mouth wide. GUARD 2 peers into it.

We're about the same age aren't we? She could be my
mother. That fucking haunts me, I'll tell you for nothing.
I'm sorry for you. I really am.

GUARD 2 *steps away.*

JOSIE. Can I have my coat please?

GUARD 2 *hands it to her.* JOSIE *puts it on. She picks up
her bag.*

JOSIE. Listen . . . If you wanted a really good night out in this
town, where would you go?

Lighting change. JOSIE *is talking to* FAY *from where she
is, their dialogue is actually taking place in the interview
room at the next visit but they stay in their own spaces,*
JOSIE *is still in the aftermath of her night out.*

FAY. Where did you go?

JOSIE. I don't want to talk about it.

FAY. Why? What happened?

JOSIE. I don't want to talk about it?

FAY. Where did you go?

Pause.

JOSIE. It was a complete fucking disaster alright?

FAY. Language.

JOSIE. What?

FAY. Watch your language!

JOSIE (*surprised*). Sorry.

FAY. Well what was it? A bar, a club? What?

JOSIE. Someone told me this wine bar was alright. *(*JOSIE
hesitates.)

FAY. Go on. What did you wear?

JOSIE *takes off her coat and turns away, tired, defeated.
She's perched, lonely at the bar.*

JOSIE. Just . . . What does it matter?

FAY. Not what you've got on?

JOSIE. What's wrong with that?

FAY. You look like . . . I don't know . . . A bank manager or something! Who's going to chat up a bank manager?

JOSIE. A man who needs a loan? I don't know. I'm not interested in being chatted up.

FAY. You're twenty-five!

JOSIE. So?

FAY. You're twenty-five!!!

JOSIE (*turning on her*). SO?!

FAY (*sits down, leaning forward, watching* JOSIE *from her cell as if* JOSIE*'s a television*). Alright then. Tell me what happened.

JOSIE. I don't want . . .

FAY. From the beginning.

JOSIE *sighs deeply. She resigns herself.*

JOSIE. Someone told me to go to this wine bar . . .

FAY (*interrupts*). Who told you?

JOSIE (*hesitates*). Just this woman. Anyway she said there was music and you didn't feel odd if you went there alone . . . But the thing is, you're going to feel odd going anywhere alone aren't you?

JOSIE *is looking round, nervous, uncomfortable.*

FAY. Jesus Christ Josie, who brought you up?

JOSIE. You know who . . .

FAY. Well she knew how to enjoy herself if anyone did!

JOSIE. Mum never went out.

Pause.

FAY. Mum did go out. I went out with Gran who also sank a few. Every Friday.

JOSIE. Yeah. With Gran. Not on your own. Have you got any idea what that's like?!

FAY. Well you don't stay on your own do you? That's the point. You talk to people.

JOSIE. People? Who?

FAY. Anyone that looks like they're into a good time!

JOSIE. So you just waltz over to some strange man and go 'Hi, I'm Josie are you into a good time?' What do you think that would . . . ?

FAY (*interrupts*). Not a man! You don't go talking to some strange man! You find a bunch of girls!

JOSIE. What do you . . . ?

FAY *is on her feet, showing her.*

FAY. You spot a bunch of women, girls' night out, not two women on their own all mousy and chilly, not a real rowdy bunch full of drink and lip, a little gaggle of girls, drinking after work maybe. Friendly but not a gang, you know? You go over, you say – (*Acting it out.*) 'Scuse me girls, I don't mean to butt in, but can you help me out? My friend Susan, (or Heather or whatever you want to call her) has stood me up and I'm looking at a night out on my own. Do you mind if I squash in at the end here, just till I finish my drink?' Then you stand the next round, then you're in for the night.

JOSIE. As easy as that is it?

FAY. What did you do? Sit there all night nursing one drink feart to talk to yourself?

JOSIE *jumps off her bar stool and advances on* FAY, *angry. They stay in separate spaces, distance between them.*

JOSIE. No, I sat there all night drinking about fourteen gin and tonics till I fell off the bar stool and the taxi driver wouldn't let me in the cab till he'd put a sheet under me. I woke up in a hedge.

FAY. What did you want to do that for!?

JOSIE. That's what every other bugger was doing! I was just joining in! Course they were doing it with their mates and I was Ms Stooky on her tod at the end of the bar but . . .

FAY. God Almighty! Didn't you talk to anyone?

JOSIE. The barman!

I don't know what I was thinking of. Why did it matter to you anyway? Why are you so set on me having a night out!?

FAY. Tell me you took your hair down and did your eyes pretty at least.

JOSIE. Why do you care!?

FAY. I thought . . . I just wanted a night out. I thought you'd go and then you'd come here and tell me about it . . . And it would be as good as going myself. Better, seeing you dressed up and lovely, dancing, imagining that, my beautiful girl. It would be like taking you out myself. Friends together.

Pause.

JOSIE. I took my hair down.

JOSIE *starts putting her hair up while talking to* FAY.

FAY. Good.

JOSIE. Is that what you did? When you were my age?

FAY. Oh when I was younger than you. When I didn't know anyone, or if I'd no-one to go out with.

JOSIE. And then what? You'd hang out with the girls?

FAY. And then you'd let some man catch your eye, or give him a smile you know? You're safe but you're not stuck with a bunch of girlfriends you can't get away from if something better comes along.

JOSIE. And that works does it?

FAY. That's how I met your Dad.

Pause.

JOSIE. Tell me?

FAY. It was at the pub disco that used to be on the corner. That
    closed in my time even but it was always out the door with
    folk back then. That wasn't my local then though, I used to
    go down the Black Cat but I'd been barred from there so . . .

JOSIE. Why?

FAY. Oh I could be wild, I don't know, dancing on tables and
    cheeking the barman, some rubbish, who cares . . . anyway
    I didn't know anyone in this place so I had to do the 'Scuse
    me girls, mind if I sit here', number. They were a great
    bunch, that's how I met your Aunty Sheila, mind her?

JOSIE. No.

FAY. Never mind. She's nothing to me now either, there's
    only been you in fifteen years. Now your Dad was at the
    bar, with his friend Mike and he caught my eye . . . and the
    first thing I thought was 'Oh I don't like the look of you',
    because he had a hard look to his face Jim, when he was
    just thinking his own thoughts, so I looked away. But when
    I looked back he was still watching me . . . and then he
    smiled. So I wasn't surprised when I found him standing at
    my shoulder and he asked me to dance . . .

    FAY *has moved completely out of her cell. She's standing
    now, lost in the memory, as if she's back there.* JOSIE *starts
    to move towards her.*

    I was wearing my black T-strap sandals and a little dress,
    jersey, burgundy. It had a split skirt and a plunge neck with
    a little raised collar, three black buttons on the front, but
    you couldn't open them, they were just for decoration . . .
    we had a laugh about that later . . . We danced, and then we
    stood at the bar and talked. It's like we were in a little world
    of our own, under a glass cover, just us . . . Mike and my
    new friends drifted by like people tapping on the glass and
    we smiled out at them like happy goldfish.

    The sun was coming up before we'd finished talking, sitting
    on the wall by the harbour, eating hot pies from the bakery.
    We'd talked all night. We slept together before we did
    anything else, I mean really slept, through till the sun was

setting again lying in his single bed with our arms round each other . . . And I swear I knew already everything we'd have together. Even you.

Pause.

Can you see it?

JOSIE. Yes.

Pause.

You don't get that from your usual night out at a club.

FAY. Och well, I wasn't thinking you'd get that. I just wanted to take you out for a drink.

Why did you go?

JOSIE. You said I looked lonely. You said I used to be different.

FAY. I expect you changed because of what happened.

JOSIE. Mum . . . Gran didn't like me going out. She liked me at home. In my room. Doing my homework. So you moved in right away?

Pause.

FAY. Near enough. He introduced me to his Mum, your Gran, the next day. Oh she was a laugh. We hit it off together straight away. They were so close, you know? She only had to take one look at his face to see he'd fallen for me, hook line and sinker, like he'd never fallen before. That was good enough for her. I was family.

JOSIE. And you had me straight after?

FAY. No. We had a couple of years on our own. We had some good times. Wild . . .

God one night, we ended up in the sea, naked in November! We nearly died. We nearly got arrested. We were coming home along the front walking and snogging at the same time . . . you know the way you do when you're warm and boozy and happy and you don't care who sees you . . . And the sea was calm as a big grey tablecloth all ready to shine when the morning slid out onto it . . . and I says to him, 'I could just slip into that now'. And he says 'I could just slip into you'. And I says, 'What, here?' And I saw the look in his eye and I says 'You'll have to catch me first' . . . and then we were running into the water . . . (filthy water it is there really! Mad!) . . . with the pebbles cutting our feet and our clothes scattered around with the oil and muck and milk cartons on the shingle.

JOSIE *and* FAY *are now face to face again. They sit down in the visiting room.*

The sounds and lights of the visiting room gradually come up around them.

Come to think of it you might have come out of that night. The timing's about right. We had good times after you came along too but, you know, babies keep you in more, or they should. (*Quiet.*) God I missed him so. I missed you. It nearly killed me.

If you leave me alone again now Josie it will kill me. Do you know that? Do you know what I'm risking here?

JOSIE *reaches out to touch* FAY*'s face.* GUARD 1 *steps up to them.*

GUARD 1 (*gentle*). No touching now.

JOSIE *and* FAY *don't even look at him.* JOSIE *lets her hand fall away from* FAY*'s face.*

FAY. You still don't remember your Dad at all Josie?

JOSIE. No. Just the smallest things . . . No. No I don't.

FAY. What I've just told you. That's the whole of it. That's all you need darling. Isn't it?

Pause.

JOSIE. O.K.

I'll be in to see you next week.

GUARD 2 (*shouting*). Time! Finish up now. That's time up everyone please.

ACT TWO

Lights up on GUARD 1 *and* GUARD 2 *sitting outside the interview room. They are eating from a large basket of fruit. They chew and peel in companionable silence for a moment.* GUARD 1 *considers the kiwi fruit in his hand.*

GUARD 1. Kangaroo gonads.

GUARD 2. What?

GUARD 1. Kiwi fruit.

GUARD 2. Kangaroos are Australian.

GUARD 1. So?

GUARD 2. Kiwis are from New Zealand.

GUARD 1. Kiwis don't have gonads do they?

GUARD 2 (*considers the kiwi, then drops it*). Little hairs cut my gums.

So how are the studies going George? The Open University.

GUARD 1. I'm surprising myself.

GUARD 2. What is it you're studying again?

GUARD 1. Moral philosophy. And theology.

GUARD 2 *snorts with laughter.*

Yes. The wife thinks it's hysterical as well. But I'm stretching myself Sheila. The brain is a muscle in a sense. It needs exercise. God knows it doesn't pay to think in here.

GUARD 1 *helps himself to another satsuma.*

Where did the fruit come from anyway?

GUARD 2. Well Josie Kerr keeps bringing it in doesn't she?

GUARD 1. Who does?

GUARD 2. Fay's daughter. She's brought her a basket every week for six months.

GUARD 1 *absorbs this then drops his satsuma.*

GUARD 1. What!?

GUARD 2. Fay won't eat it.

GUARD 1. That's not the point is it? It's her personal property. We can't eat someone's personal property!

GUARD 2. She never eats it. We put it in her room and it rots in the bowl. It's a health hazard.

GUARD 1. Have you told the daughter?

GUARD 2. It's not my business to tell her anything. She'd like to make her own mind up about things, I'm sure.

GUARD 1. Why doesn't Fay tell her?

GUARD 2. They're very close.

GUARD 1. That's my point. I gather it isn't yours?

GUARD 2. I love the way you talk George. You should be on the radio. Talking about the Queen.

GUARD 1. There was a time I would have said you were close.

GUARD 2. Who? Me and Fay?

GUARD 1. To the point of concern. Boundaries were in danger of being blurred, I would have said. But perhaps you realised that yourself. Perhaps that's why you put some distance between you, however, I'd have to say, observation of human nature being one of my main talents, I would have to say what I'm observing not so much distance as hostility.

GUARD 2. What are you saying George?

GUARD 1. You don't like Fay.

GUARD 2. Fucking hate the murdering cow.

GUARD 1. And you used to like Fay.

GUARD 2. That was before.

GUARD 1. Before what?

> GUARD 2 *says nothing for a moment. She rearranges the fruit in the basket.*

GUARD 2. You know I'm on my own with the wee one don't you George?

GUARD 1. I know she's a very lucky little girl. No-one could ever have a better mother than you Sheila.

GUARD 2. You'll make me cry George. Point is . . . Fay knew I was on my own. Or she watched that happen to me. My man slipped away from me with the afterbirth if you can handle the image George.

GUARD 1. It makes the point.

GUARD 2. And Fay knew that. She could smell the blood. When I came back to work Fay took one sniff of me and she knew. I thought no-one had ever understood what it was like to cry in the night . . .

GUARD 1. I thought you were a bit down in the mouth. New babies can do that to you, that's what I thought.

GUARD 2. She took my heart out and showed it to me. 'I know how you feel,' she said, 'Love will break you in pieces every time.' Everyone else saw a woman on her own with a kid. That was what I got pity for. Fay saw the broken heart that hurt worse than anything else. And the thing was George . . . I could have killed him. I can't tell you that wasn't a tempting idea. I wanted him dead and I wanted him back.

GUARD 1. You saw her point of view.

GUARD 2. Do you think your wife ever wishes you dead George?

GUARD 1 (*considers*). No. No she's a gentle soul. A lovely, gentle soul.

GUARD 2. Well . . . you might be surprised.

GUARD 1. My youngest daughter now, she'd stab me in my sleep. That's just her age though.

GUARD 2. You could talk to Fay. I mean they are a better kind of person our long term prisoners aren't they? Not like our B and B scum, off the street and into a cell for a couple of months' central heating and cooked food. What kind of slag drops a used tampon on the floor like a fag butt?

GUARD 1. You have to rise above it more Sheila, they're poor creatures at the end of the day.

GUARD 2. I'd like to make them eat their own filth. Talking to Fay was like talking to a favourite aunty though you know? I just about laid my head down on her and wept. Next thing you know I'm giving her my fags, we're sitting in her cell when I'm on night shift drinking hot chocolate out of my flask with a dod of whisky in it . . .

GUARD 1. Boundaries were blurred.

GUARD 2. They were rubbed out George.

GUARD 1. And what opened your eyes?

GUARD 2. One night I'm in there all evening, spilling my heart out. Next morning there's that lassie from the Islands bullied into a bloody pulp and so much junk's been moved around the prison we're finding wee packets in the drains weeks later. Everything happens when she's got my head turned. Total set up. And there's Fay sitting on a mountain of tobacco and favours that get her everything she wants for the next year. So what I'm saying is George that Fay won't tell her little girl that fruit gives her the dry boke because Fay might be needing favours off someone else soon, seeing as she can't count on anymore from me. She took me for a mug.

GUARD 1. I'd have to say you look like one there Sheila.

GUARD 2. I know. I should have known better. I do now.

GUARD 1. Disillusionment is a very aging experience in my opinion. That and personal tragedy. And no-one gets to my age without becoming an orphan at least.

GUARD 2. How old did you say you were George?

GUARD 1. However disillusion and disappointment can also be character building.

GUARD 1 helps himself to some more fruit, polishing it and stowing it in his pocket.

I shall save this for tea break, see if I can resist the chocolate biscuits.

GUARD 2. Good luck.

GUARD 1 looks at his watch as he moves off.

GUARD 1. We weren't keeping our eye on the clock there Sheila. They'll all get five minutes less visiting time. They won't be pleased.

GUARD 2 is carrying the fruit away in the opposite direction, one of them is going to let the prisoners in, the other, the visitors.

GUARD 2. Tell them disappointment is character building.

GUARD 1 laughs.

FAY walks in past one guard, JOSIE past the other. Roar of incoming visitor noise. They face each other in the middle of it. The noise dies down.

JOSIE. Mum.

FAY. Josie.

They sit opposite each other. The GUARDS walk past.

JOSIE. So how've you been?

FAY. Good. What's it like out there?

JOSIE. Cold. There was a frost this morning and it still hasn't thawed. Even the wire fence is white, sparkling.

FAY. Pretty.

JOSIE. It is. So you must be feeling the cold?

FAY. Oh I've not been too bad. Why?

JOSIE. I've been a bit under the weather. I had to go to the doctor's actually.

Both women are now keeping a very close eye on the
GUARDS' *movements.*

FAY. Did you pet? What was up?

JOSIE. Stress.

FAY. You've been working hard.

JOSIE. Well he prescribed me these tranquillisers?

FAY. Uh huh.

JOSIE. But I'm not sure if they're the right ones.

FAY (*looking at* GUARD). Hang on a minute there. Still frosty
   is it? You'll need to watch your step in those shoes, lovely
   shoes. where did you get them?

JOSIE. Oh this girl from our Glasgow branch was over in Italy
   so we all wrote out what we wanted and . . .

The GUARD *has passed,* FAY *interrupts.*

FAY. I can tell from the look of it. Get one in your hand and
   show me.

JOSIE *puts her hand in her pocket.*

Yeah you need to give your nose a wipe there.

JOSIE *gropes awkwardly in her pocket then pulls out a
tissue. She wipes her nose, holding the tissue stiff fingered,
showing* FAY *something hidden in its folds.* FAY *talks over
this.*

FAY (*nodding*). That'll do it to you, stress, you've no
   resistance to germs have you? You want to watch yourself
   in this weather.

JOSIE. They're capsules, not pills, is that . . . ?

FAY (*cutting her off*). That's great, lovely. What have you got
   them in?

JOSIE (*taking it out*). A tampons' box.

FAY. Don't show me!

JOSIE. Sorry. Sorry.

FAY. It's O.K. You don't know what you're doing. Why should you know what you're doing? That was a good idea. The tampons. Get the box in your hankie then at the end you can drop it. Can you do that?

JOSIE. Yes.

FAY. I shouldn't be asking you to do that. I only want what I need to get myself some peace. Get other people off my back you know?

JOSIE. Hey it's not a problem. It's like fiddling your duty free. No big deal. Just let me know what you need.

FAY. You've done enough . . . just some fags maybe.

JOSIE (*laughing*). No! You're killing yourself with those. Take a telling.

Pause.

FAY. Do you remember Tina?

JOSIE. Who?

FAY. Little girl, tiny she looks about twelve. She was behind us last visit.

JOSIE. I don't . . .

FAY. Well why would you, I stare at the same faces for five years you see them for five minutes, anyway she's no more bite to her than a hamster. They got her last week. I'm not even on the same block but I could hear her.

Pause. FAY *seems too distressed to go on,* JOSIE *prompts her.*

JOSIE. So what did they . . . ?

FAY (*distressed, cutting over her*). She's all cut up now you know. Down there. A fucking . . . broom handle or . . . God you wouldn't believe it. You wouldn't believe what it's like. I could hear her crying. Just 'cause she couldn't pay them off. Just a wee girl.

JOSIE. Jesus.

FAY. I wouldn't even swallow paracetamol myself.

JOSIE. I understand. You've explained it to me. I know you wouldn't.

FAY. It's worth more than money in here.

Unnoticed GUARD 2 *is close by them.*

GUARD 2. What is?

A pause FAY *and* JOSIE *both look at her, caught.*

FAY. Love.

GUARD 2. That's a beautiful thought Fay. That's lovely fruit you've been sending in to your Mum Ms Kerr. I'm sure she appreciates it. Don't you Fay?

FAY. Course I do.

GUARD 2. Lovely. Specially the kiwi fruit.

GUARD 2 *moves on.*

JOSIE. What was that about?

FAY. Nothing . . . Look at the people that come in here. (*Indicating another prisoner.*) Look at her with her daughter visiting. Two smackheads. They even look like they're the same age now. Till you came with your fresh face and your good shoes I just saw my pal Jackie and her daughter. Now I see junkies. It's another world. You shouldn't even know the way here.

JOSIE. You've given me a secret life now.

FAY. Have I?

JOSIE. I'm a woman of mystery now. No-one at work has a clue. This man, boy, that has the north east sales said to me 'What are you doing with your day off then?' I said 'Oh the usual, smuggling drugs and hanging round the jail.' His face. God. They don't expect me to come out with stuff like that you see. Not me. (*Sees* FAY*'s expression.*) What?

FAY. Sometimes . . . You've such a look of yourself.

JOSIE (*smiling*). What do you mean?

FAY. Mischievous. You were always mischievous.

JOSIE. God . . . I would love that to be me.

FAY. It is. I remember you fine. So you . . . you've told people about me? People at work?

JOSIE (*embarrassed*). No . . . No not really. They think I'm joking so . . . It's not that I wouldn't . . .

FAY. No of course.

JOSIE. It'd just be hard to explain wouldn't it?

FAY. No, no. You don't want to explain anything. So where did we go this weekend?

JOSIE. Oh I just had to do a work thing? I've been thinking about your room. How big is it? Does it have pictures on the walls?

FAY. But after. Did you go to the cinema? Did you sit in dark that smelled of popcorn and look at twenty-foot-high faces kissing?

JOSIE. No it was a dinner. Will I ever be allowed to see it?

FAY. You went to a restaurant?

JOSIE. Yes. Do you get to choose your food?

FAY. No. Did you eat that stuff I'd never heard of, what was it?

JOSIE. Couscous.

FAY. From . . .

JOSIE. Morocco.

FAY. God help us. Spicy. Is it spicy? I love spicy food.

JOSIE. I can bring you some in can't I?

FAY. Maybe . . .

JOSIE. I want to see your room. Why can't I see your room?

FAY. Because it's a prison not a hotel Josie.

JOSIE. Does no-one ever get to go to the rooms?

FAY. Maybe your solicitor, once in a blue moon.

JOSIE. I went and saw your solicitor.

Pause.

FAY. How do you know who my solicitor is?

JOSIE. It was in the newspaper report. Of your trial. He made a statement.

FAY. How did you get hold of a fifteen year old . . .

JOSIE. They've got it on microfiche. At the library.

FAY. Well . . . You have been busy haven't you? You read the newspaper report?

JOSIE. One of them.

FAY. I never read any of them.

JOSIE. So your solicitor's retired but there's a woman at the firm . . .

FAY. What did it say?

JOSIE. The newspaper?

FAY. Yes.

JOSIE. There were a few articles . . . Reports on the . . . what happened. Reports on the trial.

FAY. How bad was it?

JOSIE. You didn't say what happened. Did you? You stood in the dock and you didn't say a word. They've got a picture of you. An artist's impression. You look very pretty and very sad.

FAY. I don't remember any of it.

JOSIE. Have you ever told anyone what happened?

Pause.

FAY. No.

JOSIE. Will you tell me?

Pause.

FAY. You don't need to know that.

JOSIE. I feel like I do.

FAY. Pushy. You always were a pushy wee madam.

JOSIE. I'm very goal orientated. These days I feel like I could do anything Mum. I feel great. We could just have a chat. In your room.

FAY. Who?

JOSIE. You and me and your solicitor. A private meeting, so we could really talk.

FAY. Oh you think they'd let us do that?

JOSIE. We could ask. I could ask.

FAY. Oh you'll be writing to the governor now will you?

JOSIE. Why not? I'm going to find out the best way to do it. I thought I'd ask him today.

JOSIE *indicates* GUARD 1.

FAY. You don't want to talk to him.

JOSIE. He's got a kind face.

FAY. He's got the key to the door, but he won't let you use it.

JOSIE. He reminds me of someone . . .

FAY. How many keys have you got?

JOSIE. What?

FAY. House key? Car key?

JOSIE. God I don't know . . . eight or nine . . . Why . . . ?

FAY. I read something in a magazine. It shows how you've advanced in life how many keys you have. How many doors you can open. He can open over two hundred.

JOSIE. But they're not his doors.

FAY. Might as well be. Cock of the walk. A fox in the henhouse. Yeah he's got a kind face. He's nothing but kind. Surround one man in women and he doesn't ever need to be anything but kind does he? They'll do everything else. He can just lie back in his armchair and put his paper over his face and be kind can't he? They'll run about clucking, being busy, being bossy, nagging and pushing and being all the bad things he never has to flex a muscle to be . . .

JOSIE. You don't like him?

FAY. He's alright.

JOSIE. Then I'll talk to him.

FAY. Don't.

JOSIE. But why not?

FAY. What are we talking about this for? Why are we wasting time with this? I want to know what you've been up to. What happened with that man you said you liked the look of? At the gym?

JOSIE. That was nothing! That was just . . . Look I'm trying to ask you something important Mum, can we just drop this obsession with my love life for once!

FAY. I am only forty-five years old and I will never make love again. Ever.

Pause.

JOSIE. You don't know that.

FAY. What are my chances?

GUARD 1 *walks past, they both watch.* FAY *starts to laugh.* JOSIE *joins in.*

You see you would, wouldn't you? And there's some that do, believe me.

JOSIE. He's shagging women in here!?

FAY. Oh not George! There were a couple of girls used to go back of the kitchens with the guy that was here two years ago though. More than a couple. Face down over the potato peelings for an extra phone call or a change from the telly . . . I'd rather shove wasps up my arse . . .

Pause.

JOSIE. Your solicitor retired but there's a woman in the same firm. Janice Fraser.

FAY. Who's she to me?

JOSIE. She said I looked like you.

Pause.

FAY. Its just paperwork and heartache!

JOSIE. Janice says . . .

FAY. Fifteen years Josie! If there was a loophole do you not think I'd've wriggled my way out of it by now?!

Pause.

JOSIE. I didn't mean to upset you.

FAY. Then do what I tell you will you? Leave it alone!

JOSIE. But no-one really knows what happened. No-one but you.

FAY. And that's the way I want it! Take a telling!

Pause.

JOSIE. I think he hurt you terribly. Terribly.

Pause.

FAY. It's all long gone Josie.

JOSIE. I just think you should let me . . .

FAY. You want to see my room!?

What do you see out your window these mornings Josie? Frost sparkle, outside where it's cold and you're warm under your duvet? Know what I see? (*Leaning closer to* JOSIE, *assaulting her with the image*.) Just a slice of sky, a knife-shaped piece of cloud or blue to cut me to pieces, a razor edge of view. I press myself up to the window to see it, push against it shredding my flesh, forcing the sight of it into the wound that's already there, just a slice of blue sky all outlined in brick.

Sound and lighting start to change, they're occupying their private imagined space again.

And I've lived with the smell of backing up toilets and boiled food. For years! Till it's the smell of my skin. Can't you smell it? It would be easier if there was no sky at all. It would be easier if they buried me in the ground.

I watch pigeons fly past. I hate pigeons so much I'd like to grab their maggoty little warty-toed legs and smash them on the stones. Look at them fluttering free over the only bit of view I'll ever have! Ugly feathery little bastards!

There are so many of us squashed in here, the damp that runs down the plaster smells of our sweat. Why don't they put me in a dungeon? Why don't they lock me in a real cell, iron bars, chains, I wouldn't feel so crazy. They've put me in hell and stuck curtains round the view and planted fucking geraniums for the visitors. They've made me a madwoman.

That's what it's like.

JOSIE. I'm sorry.

FAY. I know.

JOSIE. I didn't . . . I'm sorry.

FAY. You take me back home. Back home. In from work in time for you coming in from school . . . What did I have working from you? . . . Come on Josie.

Pause.

JOSIE. I'd get a chocolate biscuit.

FAY. Penguins were your favourite. And it's a treat for tea. What is it?

JOSIE. Chips.

FAY. From?

JOSIE. The Golden Plaice. On the front.

FAY. Best chips. Hot and crisp.

JOSIE. Two fish suppers . . . one . . . what was it? One smoked sausage supper. Salt and sauce on the fish just salt on the sausage.

FAY. Now that I couldn't remember! That's amazing Josie!

JOSIE. Who ate the sausage supper?

FAY. . . . Your Dad did of course.

Pause.

JOSIE. How can I remember something like that and not remember him? I can't see him. I try and try and there's nothing . . . Except . . . Brushing his teeth in the sink . . . and lying on the sofa . . .

FAY. Do you ever wear earrings Josie?

JOSIE. No.

FAY. Feel your ears.

JOSIE *does so.*

There's little hard knots in there aren't there?

JOSIE (*wondering*). Yes.

FAY. Haven't you ever wondered about that?

JOSIE. I thought they were just part of my ears.

FAY. You didn't always come straight home from school you know.

JOSIE. I didn't?

FAY. No. I got a phone call. From the jewellers on the High Street. I said you couldn't get your ears pierced. You were too young. But you were crazy for earrings. You used to sellotape milk bottle tops to your ears. But I wasn't having it. So you took all your pocket money to school and then got a bus up the High Street to the jewellers and tried to get them to put studs in.

JOSIE *fingers her ears.*

JOSIE. And they did?

FAY. No of course they didn't! You were too young. They phoned me to come and get you. Aw the greitin face you had on when I came in the door.

JOSIE (*ears*). So, how come . . . ?

FAY. I told them to do it. If you were that determined. I mean you were only seven. You'd never even got on a bus yourself before. I didn't even know how you found your way there. I said if you're old enough to do that you're maybe old enough for earrings after all. And then I bought you your first drink.

JOSIE. You didn't!

FAY. I did. It was a babycham. You loved it.

We had it outside the pub. I got an orange juice so they were O.K. with it and you got my babycham. We sat there like a couple of grown-up ladies talking jewellery. Oh don't tell me you don't remember that Josie! You were so happy!

JOSIE. I don't know . . . (*Thinking hard.*) I remember being outside a pub one time . . . but . . . I was with Gran. That's it, I was with Gran and we were looking for you . . . or were we looking for Dad? Were we looking for you and Dad?

FAY (*changes the subject*). Oh you might have been. I don't remember that one.

Pause.

JOSIE. Did he drink?

FAY. What kind of a question's that?

JOSIE. I was just wondering . . .

FAY. Course he drank. We both drank. What's wrong with that?

JOSIE. Nothing I just . . .

FAY. We weren't fucking alchys if that's what you mean.

Pause.

JOSIE. I keep upsetting you.

FAY. I'm not upset.

I just can't believe you don't remember about the earrings.

JOSIE. I do! I mean I remember wanting them.

FAY. Oh you wanted them alright.

JOSIE. Well why not? You had earrings.

FAY *laughs with delight.*

FAY. That's exactly what you said! Why have you not worn earrings since then?

JOSIE. I don't know.

FAY. I bought you a pair every birthday and every Christmas. You should get your ears pierced again.

JOSIE. Yeah maybe I will.

FAY. No really, you should. Do it this week. Do it before you come again. Alright?

JOSIE. Alright.

FAY. Then we can talk earrings again. Like grown up ladies.

JOSIE. I think I do remember Dad . . .

Pause.

FAY. What do you remember?

JOSIE. I'm coming downstairs . . . The house is really quiet.

Pause.

FAY. Well that never happened did it? It was never quiet in our house.

JOSIE. I'm coming downstairs and there isn't a sound and I'm going to be very grown up . . . I'm going to boil the kettle and make a cup of tea. Did I make you a cup of tea Sunday mornings?

Pause.

FAY. You were a good girl.

JOSIE. And I see a broken mug.

FAY. Don't look. Just don't look Josie. You don't need to see anything.

JOSIE. But this is what I'm telling you! That's where I can see him!

FAY *says nothing, she's now very tense.*

He's on the sofa . . . and he's . . . snoring. He's made a mess. He's made a mess all over the sofa. What's he done? He's thrown up? He's pissed himself? He's drunk.

FAY. Don't look at him.

JOSIE. He's drunk. He hasn't got the sense to brush his teeth in the bathroom. He's going to spit in the dirty dishes in the kitchen sink. What's his toothbrush doing by the kitchen sink?

FAY. It was a pot scourer. Just forget this Josie, it's not who he was . . .

JOSIE. He hit you didn't he?

Pause.

FAY. Is that what you remember?

JOSIE. I know he must have hurt you.

Pause.

FAY. Everyone said he was a very peaceful man. Very kind. He just sat in his chair and read his paper. No trouble to anyone.

Pause.

JOSIE. What did he do?

FAY. You're a pushy wee madam, though I'm sure that's how you're wearing designer shoes.

JOSIE. Just tell me some . . .

FAY (*interrupts*). You know what, I've been thinking. You should buy a place round here.

JOSIE. Buy a house?

FAY. Yeah, it's no good for you. All this travelling about. You'll never make a life for yourself.

Pause.

JOSIE. I like my life.

FAY. Then what are you doing here?

Pause.

JOSIE. It's a big step that's all.

FAY. You could still go off to California couldn't you? It would just be something to come back to.

Pause.

You hate that idea don't you?

JOSIE. No I just . . .

FAY. Aw Jesus you're going to leave aren't you? You're moving on. You've bought your ticket. You're off to fucking San Diego aren't you?

JOSIE. I'm not!

FAY. Of course you are! What do you want to be hanging round here for. Spending your time off sitting in a jail when you could be flying round the world . . .

JOSIE. I just told you how I feel about that! Weren't you listening to me?

FAY. You're going to leave me.

JOSIE. I'm not.

FAY. You are . . .

JOSIE. I'm not! Mum . . . Mum . . . (*Forcing* FAY *to look at her.*) I love you. I can't believe I found you. I can't believe what you're giving me. I won't ever leave you now. Not ever.

Pause. FAY *looks at her, fighting tears*.

FAY. But you'll get some bloody solicitor dragging out all the old papers and newspapers and evidence . . . making me remember all that . . .

JOSIE (*intense*). I won't. I won't do that to you again. I'm sorry. I'll never do that again. I promise.

FAY *starts to recover*

FAY. O.K . . . O.K . . . Thanks darling . . . And you'll get your ears pierced?

JOSIE (*laughing*). You don't give up, do you?

FAY (*smiling*). Tell me about your meal. Where did you go?

JOSIE. It was just work.

FAY. Aw Josie!

JOSIE. An Indian . . .

FAY. Pakora and chicken madras. That was my Friday night favourite. My mouth's watering. I'd chew my way through a door for that now. What did you wear?

JOSIE. My black trouser suit.

FAY. What is it with you and black?

JOSIE. I suit black.

FAY. You suit red.

Show me where your neckline was.

JOSIE *points*.

That's lovely. You see you've got a lovely figure Josie.

JOSIE. Thank you Mum.

FAY. Right. I can picture you, that's nearly a good night out. So did you meet anyone nice?

JOSIE. It was work!

FAY. Alright did you meet anyone I could get a snog off?

JOSIE. You know you might go for my boss . . .

FAY. Would I?

JOSIE. He's very married . . .

FAY. That's O.K. I haven't really got any space in my diary.
What's he look like?

JOSIE. Wee bit grey here . . . (*temples*) . . . big, tall . . .
carrying a wee bit of weight but carrying it you know?

FAY. Solid.

JOSIE. Yeah. He makes you laugh and he's very . . . warm.
Warm is how he is. Warm hands.

FAY. Aw Jesus. Warm hands.

Pause while FAY *savours this.*

Well . . . Maybe we could all have a drink together sometime
eh? And you'll say, 'This is my mother,' and I'll shake his
big warm hand and he'll buy me . . . a martini . . . I wouldn't
shame you by asking for a vodka and iron bru . . . and we'll
get to know each other.

Pause.

Wouldn't that be good?

JOSIE. Yes.

FAY. Time to go soon. Tell you what, get yourself chips for
tea. Eat them when they're hot, straight out the paper.

JOSIE. What will you have?

FAY. Don't worry about it.

The lighting slowly changes, The GUARDS *become visible
again slowly walking back down the room like figures
underwater.* JOSIE *and* FAY *move back to their seats.*

Don't forget your hanky.

JOSIE. My . . . ? Oh yeah.

*JOSIE casually gets the tampon packet out of her bag. It's
wrapped in a tissue. She lets it drop. Both women glance
quickly to make sure the* GUARDS *haven't seen.*

FAY. Camera saw but they didn't. As long as they don't run the tape. Sometimes they do sometimes they don't. (*Louder.*) You dropped your hanky.

JOSIE. No that's yours.

FAY. Is it? (*Quiet.*) If it's mine it'll be a bit of bog roll. We don't run to Kleenex in here you know.

JOSIE. Sorry.

FAY. Next time. You'll get the hang of it.

She scoops it up. The GUARDS *don't seem to have seen.* GUARD 1 *strolls past them. The lighting state has returned to what it was,* GUARDS *are moving normally.*

GUARD 1 (*calling*). Finish up now please!

The growing noise of people leaving the visiting room. Sense of their movement all around.

FAY. So listen, I'm sorry about . . . If you need to go off travelling again . . .

JOSIE. I don't.

FAY. It's fine. As long as I knew you were coming back. As long as I knew. I get scared of losing you again.

JOSIE. I'm not going anywhere.

FAY. You could send me postcards. Take photographs. Have you been to Paris?

JOSIE. Yeah couple of times

FAY. Aw God what's it like Josie?

GUARD 1. Time now everyone! Time please!

JOSIE. Not a patch on coming here.

FAY and JOSIE *get up.*

FAY. Tell me about it next time.

JOSIE. I will.

FAY. And thank you sweetheart. Thank you.

JOSIE. Don't worry about anything. O.K?

FAY (*smiling*). O.K.

JOSIE. I love you Mum.

> FAY *blows a kiss and walks off smiling.* JOSIE *watches her go. When she turns round* GUARD 2 *is waiting for her.*

GUARD 2. Well I think you know what we have to do now Ms Kerr.

JOSIE. You won't find anything.

GUARD 2. No. Not on you. But you never know.

> JOSIE *follows* GUARD 2. FAY *is back in her cell. She's humming, happy.*

> JOSIE *just stands as* GUARD 2 *conducts her search, she knows the routine now, anticipating* GUARD 2's *moves. After a moment* GUARD 2 *starts talking conversationally.*

GUARD 2. I know where she'll have got you to about now.

> JOSIE *says nothing.*

She'll be making you feel like you owe her the world by now, and you don't want to give her anything anymore but you can't see how you could live with yourself if you don't.

She does it to everyone.

> GUARD 1 *enters* FAY's *cell.* FAY *stands up, she slumps, her good mood draining out of her.*

GUARD 1. Now you know I hate to do this Fay.

> GUARD 2 *pauses, her hands in* JOSIE's *hair, her face close to hers.*

GUARD 2. She will rip you apart. I am not kidding you. She will rip you apart.

> *At the exact moment* GUARD 2 *stops speaking* GUARD 1 *launches himself at* FAY's *room. He starts to tear it apart.*

> GUARD 2 *continues her search of* JOSIE.

FAY (*quiet, tearful*). Please George no. Just let me . . . Please don't. Please.

She can make no move to stop him. Pictures are ripped from their frames, bedding hurled on the floor. Clothes and books scattered.

The two searches finish at the same moment. GUARD 1 *finds the package of pills. He pulls it out, opens the tampon box and looks in it.*

GUARD 2 (*to* JOSIE). See you next week I suppose.

JOSIE. Yes. You will.

GUARD 1. Oh dear, oh dear, oh dear.

GUARD 1 *leaves.*

FAY *is slumped on the floor of her wrecked room. After a moment she gets up and starts to tidy distractedly, it's hopeless.* FAY *stops again. She starts to pace again, muttering to herself.*

FAY. A bad day, a bad day, a bad day. I can't have a bad day, can't, where's my fags, where's my fags, where's my fags?!

FAY *searches the wreckage frantically. Turns and screams at the door.*

Where's my fags! Give me my fags back you bastard! Give me my fucking fags!

The sounds of the prison surge up around her, someone is thumping heavily on the wall, voices screaming at her to shut up.

FAY *slumps again.*

A week later. JOSIE *is waiting outside the interview room.*

GUARD 1 *is watching her sympathetically.* JOSIE *approaches him hesitantly.*

JOSIE. You didn't call my name out.

GUARD 1. And that is?

JOSIE. Josie . . . Josie Kerr.

GUARD 1 *looks at his list.*

GUARD 1. Have you got a visitor's order?

JOSIE. No but . . . I thought maybe there was a mistake. I mean I've been coming regularly.

GUARD 1. You're Fay's daughter aren't you?

JOSIE. Yes.

GUARD 1. Ah. Well. You should have been told really. Fay is on punishment.

JOSIE. What?

GUARD 1. No visits for three months.

JOSIE. But . . .

GUARD 1. Unauthorised medication found in cell.

Pause.

JOSIE. She wouldn't do that . . . You don't know . . . She wouldn't.

GUARD 1. It was disappointing. But evidence is evidence.

JOSIE. Three months.

GUARD 1. Yes.

JOSIE. You can't do that. You can't.

GUARD 1. That is our current policy after a discovery of this kind.

JOSIE. But you can't! She needs . . . I have to see her. I have to.

GUARD 1. No. Not today.

JOSIE. But they can't . . . you can't do this! I've come to see her!

GUARD 1. Not possible I'm afraid. You could write her a note.

JOSIE. I'll write to someone! I'll write and complain!

GUARD 1. You can do that too.

JOSIE. There must be some way I can see her today. There must be some way!

GUARD 1. No. Now don't get yourself upset.

JOSIE. I'm not upset!

GUARD 1. Of course you are. She's your Mum. You're upset.

JOSIE. But you're not are you! You're not! You see this all the time don't you!

Pause.

GUARD 1. There's an implied judgment there that's a tad unrealistic if I may say so.

JOSIE. Well fuck you!!

JOSIE *collapses, hand to her face.*

JOSIE. I'm sorry. I'm sorry.

GUARD 1 *says nothing.*

JOSIE. I'm really sorry. I just . . . Does she know I'm here?

GUARD 1. I'd say no. I can usually tell. The women show it, if they're missing their kids. Tears them to bits.

I was in a male prison before this. They just lost touch completely. Kids might as well have been posted to the moon. But the women, even five-, eight-year sentences, they're on the phone, being Mum.

It's only natural. It's a bond like no other.

JOSIE. I can leave a message with you? A letter?

GUARD 1. Of course you can.

JOSIE *starts to look in her handbag, finds a pen.*

I tell you the thing I like about working with women, the smell. You open one of the doors in the men's prison and the stink'll knock you back against the wall. Not here. They all save up, buy themselves air fresheners, soap . . . Your Mum keeps her room like a little palace. Lovely and fresh.

JOSIE. Have you got any paper?

GUARD 1 *finds her some.*

GUARD 1. And you know where you are with the women. They don't bottle things up. If they're angry, they let you know it. If they're unhappy, you can see it straight away. Not like the men.

Women are like dogs, doesn't matter how much they've been kicked they'll still turn towards kindness. Treat women prisoners with kindness and they'll go where they're told, come when they're asked and see the sense of it. And you know if they're pleased or miserable as easy as if they had a tail to wag.

Sounds daft but I've been a student of human nature for thirty years. And I've a wife and three daughters at home. I know whereof I speak.

It all seems perfectly normal. They're just like any women anywhere in here.

JOSIE *is writing.*

I've always found your mother a very easy woman to talk to. An intelligent woman. She must be proud of you.

Pause.

JOSIE. I don't know.

GUARD 1. I'm sure of it. You've made something of yourself. It's good to see.

Pause.

Of course if she'd killed you she'd probably only be serving ten years, less if she got you when you were younger.

JOSIE *looks up, startled.*

JOSIE. I'm sorry?!

GUARD 1. Oh don't worry about me. I'm just rambling on as usual. Pondering life's inconsistencies as you do. It's too much time without natural sunlight, that's my theory, deprive a man of sunlight and his mind will go underground and turn to brooding. I'm not certain these fluorescent tubes aren't carcinogenic. You could imagine they might be couldn't you?

JOSIE. What are you talking about, if she killed me . . . ? What do you mean?

GUARD 1. If a man kills his girlfriend he'll get a ten stretch. If a woman kills her kid she'll probably only serve as long as that poor little scrap ever lived, two years, three . . . If a woman kills her man it's life and there's an end to it. That's how it is. I'm sure you can find me a list of exceptions but statistically, on average, as a general rule that is how the courts rate the value of life.

Now mind you I'm not saying they're wrong to dish out long sentences. Maybe the fairest solution is to increase all the other sentences. Life for a life, any life, there's a certain biblical symmetry and sense of natural justice about that isn't there? But it's not for me to say.

My eldest girl is just a bit younger than you. Training to be a solicitor. We're very proud.

JOSIE. I still don't know what you're talking about.

GUARD 1 *is suddenly speaking to her with intimate intensity.*

GUARD 1. There is nothing fair about any of it. You will not find fairness here no matter how hard you search. I earn a living here Ms Kerr. I have to understand the realities of what I deal with. I have to crawl underground and live under strip lighting to feed my family. You have no idea. You see a woman. You see your mother. The surface looks like everything you'd expect but these walls swallow people. It's just a thought but you might want to turn round and never come back. You will never understand. You keep the law and pay your taxes so you never have to understand. Never have to think about it. Keep it that way or it'll drive you crazy. Just a suggestion inspired by long experience. You see?

For an answer JOSIE *hands him her letter.*

GUARD 1 *takes it. He reads it in front of her.*

His tone has reverted to his usual pleasant chat.

That's beautifully put Ms Kerr, I'm sure that'll cheer her up.

Closed visiting room, two weeks later.

GUARD 2 *is standing close to* JOSIE *talking quietly. We have a sense of a much smaller claustrophobic space.*

GUARD 2. Look . . . She's got to be on punishment otherwise it's like she's just got away with it. She had drugs in her room. For all we know you brought them to her. We will be watching you. Do you understand?

JOSIE *nods, tense.*

GUARD 2. To be honest I didn't think she was serious. They love to act it up you know, all of them but she's really gone for it . . .

GUARD 1 *comes in gently guiding* FAY. GUARD 2 *'switches off' and goes to stand by the wall with her hands behind her back. Both* GUARD 1 *and* 2 *remain very close to* FAY *and* JOSIE *throughout this scene.*

FAY *is pale, emaciated, very wobbly on her feet.* GUARD 1 *guides her to a chair.* JOSIE *is shaken by the sight of her.*

JOSIE. My God!

FAY *gives her a weak smile.*

FAY. Hi there.

JOSIE. Jesus what have you done to yourself?

FAY. I don't think the diet's working Josie.

JOSIE. What have you done?

GUARD 2. Hunger strike.

JOSIE. I didn't know. I didn't know.

GUARD 2. It's the only reason we're letting you near her.

GUARD 1. There is a mental health issue . . .

GUARD 2. She should be left without visits another month but we can't have another suicide on our hands.

FAY. God it's nice to see you.

GUARD 1. Now this will be a closed visit . . .

GUARD 2. In here.

GUARD 1. Under supervision.

GUARD 2. With us.

JOSIE. You've got to eat something. You've got to eat something right now!

FAY. Och I've no appetite these days.

GUARD 1. Are you prepared to accept those conditions?

JOSIE (*distracted*). Yes! (*to* FAY) You have to eat.

GUARD 2. Don't get too upset, we'll have to cut it short if you're getting each other upset.

JOSIE *turns to the* GUARDS.

JOSIE. Where's the fruit? I brought some fruit in for her. She can have that can't she?

FAY (*cutting over this*). Josie! I don't like fruit darling, I can't eat it.

JOSIE. What?

FAY. It's too acid. It hurts my stomach.

JOSIE. Why did you never tell me?

FAY. I didn't have the heart to pet. You thought you were doing me good.

JOSIE. Well . . . What would you eat?

FAY. I could murder an ice cream sundae.

JOSIE. I've got some chocolate in my bag.

FAY. I could try a bit of that I suppose.

JOSIE (*to* GUARDS). Please can I give it to her. Please.

GUARD 1. We'll have to check your bag again Josie.

JOSIE hands it over. GUARD 1 *looks through it.*

FAY. I know it's not good for me but it's just what I fancy.

GUARD 1 *finds the chocolate bar and hands it* GUARD 2. *She unwraps it and sniffs it.*

JOSIE. Oh for God's sake!

FAY. If she licks it I'll not touch it even if it saves my life.

GUARD 2 *hands the chocolate to* FAY. *She tries to break a piece off, she can't.* JOSIE *moves to help her. Both* GUARDS *step forward.*

GUARD 2. Hey!

GUARD 1. No touching now Josie.

JOSIE. Oh fuck's sake! Come on then! Search me again! Come on! What do you want? You think I've got a bag of cocaine in my knickers!? Come on then! Take a look!

JOSIE is advancing on them, pretending to pull down her clothes.

GUARD 2. Get back please.

GUARD 1. Calm down now Josie.

JOSIE. You think I've got a razor blade behind my ear? Go on take a look! Go on!

She drops her head, shaking her hair at them.

FAY. Josie, calm down and behave yourself.

They all look at her.

JOSIE. I just want to help her eat. Please let me help her eat.

GUARD 2. I'll do it.

FAY. I'd bite your fucking fingers off Sheila.

GUARD 1. O.K. well I'll . . .

FAY (*cutting over him*). I'd spit it on the floor.

Pause.

GUARD 1. Alright then Josie. Just till she's eaten something.

JOSIE *crosses over to* FAY. *She crouches beside her. She breaks off a bit of chocolate and feeds it to Fay.* FAY *chews slowly and swallows. She starts to giggle.*

FAY. God almighty that feels like a high. Can you believe it? Stoned on a sugar rush Josie. That's lovely.

JOSIE. Have another bit, come on.

She feeds her another piece.

FAY. Mmmm. Give me a wee rest now. That's lovely though.

JOSIE. Do you like it?

FAY. Mmmm. Can I get a drink of water?

JOSIE *looks round.*

JOSIE. In my bag. You must've seen it.

GUARD 2 *looks in* JOSIE'*s handbag. She pulls out a bottle of water. She takes the top off.*

FAY. Watch her spit in it.

GUARD 2 *hands over the water without comment.* JOSIE *helps* FAY *take a drink.*

This is great, waited on hand and foot. It's worth being at death's door just for the service.

JOSIE. Do you want some more chocolate?

FAY. Maybe in a minute.

GUARD 1. Move away now please Josie.

Reluctantly JOSIE *moves away from* FAY.

FAY. So what have you been up to darling? Snogged anyone decent?

JOSIE. They didn't even tell me you weren't allowed visits anymore.

FAY. Och they never tell anyone anything. Tell me something else. Have you bought any new clothes? Have you been anywhere nice? You're looking awfully peaky Josie.

JOSIE. I'm O.K. I missed you.

FAY. Now. Don't get me greiting. We'll not be a little cabaret for George and Sheila will we? Tell me something cheerful.

JOSIE *can't speak for a moment. She's fighting tears.*

FAY. Come on darling. Please. We'll not get much time.

JOSIE. Look.

She shows her ears. She's got studs in.

FAY. Oh well done! Well done! Did it hurt?

JOSIE. No.

FAY. You never cried the first time.

JOSIE. I went to a jewellers on the High Street. I don't know if it was the same place. I didn't remember it. But the Italian restaurant's still there.

FAY. You went back!

JOSIE. Yes.

FAY. What was it like?

JOSIE. Small . . . I remembered . . . odd things . . . chimney pots and trees. The shops are all different. Different kind of windows.

FAY. Did you . . . go to the house?

JOSIE *nods.*

JOSIE. The garden was all overgrown.

Pause.

FAY. Oh that would've annoyed him.

JOSIE. The roses are still there.

FAY. Good.

Pause.

FAY. Did you go to the beach?

JOSIE. Yes. I walked up and down for hours. I watched the tide come in. Nothing came in with it, not even seaweed. My shoes were full of sand.

FAY. They always were, and your pockets. It was hell on the washing machine.

How did it feel?

JOSIE (*smiles*). I felt old.

FAY. Och what rubbish.

JOSIE. I wanted you there.

Pause.

FAY. Och well, it'd be a bit cold walking on the beach today wouldn't it?

JOSIE. Listen . . . I've done something . . . I know you asked me not to but . . . I . . . we can't go on like this. We can't.

FAY. What have you done?

JOSIE. Janice . . . Janice Fraser, your new solicitor? She reckons you can appeal.

FAY. Appeal what?

JOSIE. Your sentence.

Pause.

FAY. No way Josie.

JOSIE. Listen to me! You never had a psychiatric evaluation.

FAY. I told you not to do this. You promised me.

JOSIE. No-one knows what happened. No-one. It's all in your head.

FAY. Everyone knows what I'm sentenced for Josie.

JOSIE. What Janice wants to do . . .

FAY. Janice isn't getting near me . . .

JOSIE. Listen! Just listen to me! Let me help you!

FAY. I don't want this Josie!

GUARD 2 (*cold*). Are you getting upset Fay? Do you need to stop?

FAY (*panicking*). That's not time. That's never time.

GUARD 2. She's getting upset.

FAY. I'm not!

JOSIE. She's not.

FAY. We're fine.

> JOSIE *turns all her attention back on* FAY.

JOSIE. We're O.K. Aren't we? Just listen. Please just listen.

> *Pause.*

FAY. Alright.

JOSIE. What we have to do. What you have to do . . . with us . . . is go back over the evidence, piece by piece, and talk it through . . . with Janice and a trained psychiatrist, I can be there too if you want. There are things that would be considered mitigating factors. Things that no-one got you to talk about. What stresses you were under. What he did to you. How he made you feel. We need to know what you were thinking, how you felt when . . . it happened.

FAY. Why? Why do you need that? Why do I have to talk about that?

JOSIE. Because then you can make them understand. We can lodge an appeal. We can tell them.

FAY. Tell them what?

JOSIE. Tell them your side of it. No-one knows your side of it. You shouldn't be here.

FAY. How do you know?

JOSIE. I know. I remember you.

FAY. You shouldn't be doing this Josie. You should be living your life.

JOSIE. I gave up my job.

FAY. What?

JOSIE. I'm getting something part time. In town. Janice can't work on this 24/7 but I can. I can do all the searches, all the paperwork. I can work at this day and night till it's done.

FAY. Oh Jesus what're you doing giving up your job?!

FAY slumps back. JOSIE *steps towards her. The* GUARDS *step in to stop her.* JOSIE *gives an exclamation of frustration.*

JOSIE. Oh for Christ's sake! You getting all this? Are you enjoying the show?

She moves as near to FAY *as they'll allow. She bends down to look up into* FAY*'s face.*

JOSIE. The day I couldn't get in to see you I went home and I just took to my bed. I was paralysed. I woke up the next morning and there wasn't a thought in my head. I just lay there looking at the bit of sky I could see out the window, watching the birds, the tops of the trees. Watching the light come and go. I hardly moved. I couldn't have told you what I was thinking. It was like . . . I'd started to remember who I was. To feel like myself and then I couldn't talk to you. And I was nothing, not even who I thought I was before. I'm nothing without you.

FAY. That's rubbish Josie.

JOSIE. That's what you said to me. We need each other.

FAY. Stop this Josie. Not in front of them. I don't want them listening to this.

JOSIE. I don't care! Listen, I have always been good at what I do. Always. You ask my Gran. I was a star pupil, I got any job I went for. I always get what I go for and this is what I'm going for now, whatever it takes. I'm twenty-five Mum. You can't tell me how to live my life.

Pause.

FAY. You see . . . What I thought . . . What I was daydreaming about was first you'd have a bit of fun . . . You'd give me a taste of tequila, remind me of that pain in your toes when they're crammed into real fuck-off heels and you've been dancing in them . . .

JOSIE. I can't wear stilettos.

FAY. Aw I'd get you in stilettos . . . And you wouldn't really tell me about the men because I'm your mother and it's embarrassing but I'd know, I'd see the glow on you, I'd be happy for you . . . And then I thought . . . Maybe, after a while, after a great few years of fun, there'd be someone, someone I could get to know from the way you told me, how he looked, how he made you feel, how desperate it was to be in love with him but wonderful 'cause he loved you back . . . stupid stuff . . . like watching b.movie actors kissing . . . but I'd see you, in my head, happy, like I was . . . And I thought . . . Maybe he'll love all of you. Maybe he'll come in sometime to visit . . . And I'll tell you what I think. Tell you if he's good enough for you. And maybe if he is . . . there'd be kids. Maybe I'd get to see kids. Maybe I'd watch your life. A family. A life . . . My life.

Isn't it stupid what you imagine when you've nothing else to do?

JOSIE. I am never going to wear stilettos. I am never going to wear red. I don't know if I'll ever want to be in love. But I can do this Mum. I can do this!

Pause.

FAY. Oh I want to get out of here.

JOSIE. I know.

FAY. I want to walk down the street and hear traffic, and go into shops and buy ice cream and cigarettes and fucking fruit! I want to walk on the beach! I want to eat hot chips out of paper! I want a proper drink! I want to kiss a man with a moustache! I want to take a crap in a bathroom that smells of soap and water not other people's shit! I don't want to hear doors banging and yelling and breathe air that stinks of other people's bad teeth! I want to look out a window just once, just once and see a view I've never seen before! I want to get out!

JOSIE. I know. I'm going to get you out.

FAY. You're not! You're not! You're going to get me paperwork and memories that'd make my head bleed! All I want is for you to take me dancing with you! That's all I've got! All I've got now is your life.

You're squashing your life down till it's no bigger than my cell.

JOSIE. Good, then I'll fit in beside you and you'll never be alone again. Neither of us will.

A long pause. FAY is just looking at JOSIE, a very, very painful decision is forming in her.

FAY (*quiet*). Well I can't let you do that darling. That's no good to either of us.

JOSIE. You can't stop me Mum. I've made up my mind.

Another pause. FAY looks at GUARD 2.

FAY. Well are you ever getting the last laugh. Take me back to my room then you cow, go on.

FAY struggles to get up.

JOSIE. What are you doing?

FAY. I don't want you to come and visit me anymore Josie. It's not good for you.

JOSIE. What do you mean?

FAY. I don't want you coming in here anymore! Go away!

JOSIE. You can't do that.

FAY. Yes I can. They can make me get up when they want and lock me up when they want and pull me to bits when they want but they can't make me eat and they can't make me see anyone I don't want to see. Those are my rights. Aren't they Sheila?

JOSIE. You're protecting him aren't you! I know you are! You're not telling us what happened! What did he do to you!?

FAY. You don't remember?

JOSIE. No!

FAY. No. You don't remember him at all. He read you bedtime stories, every night he could. Girls' stories about princesses and ponies. He fucking hated reading. He did it 'cause you loved it. Can't you remember him sitting on your bed?

JOSIE. No.

FAY. Now he's taken you out. He's working late, I'm out with the girls, he's taken you along. Can you see his toolbox Josie? You'll be round at someone else's house and he'll be up a ladder fixing their wiring and chatting to the woman and you're sitting by his feet, chewing the toffee you've been given and in a minute he'll ask you to pass him up . . .

JOSIE (*quiet*). The pliers.

FAY. There you go. You're the electrician's mate. (*The really hard bit now.*) Now it's first thing in the morning. The house is all quiet. I must be out. Where's your Dad going to be if I'm already out because I'm too angry to stay inside four walls without smashing them? Where will he be?

Pause.

JOSIE. On the sofa.

FAY. Asleep on the sofa with his drinking head waking him up all cross and thirsty. I'm not coming home, I'm probably already in the early pub by the docks, swallowing my rage.

I'll not be home till tea or till you and your Gran come looking for me.

We didn't drink so much though. No more than a lot of folk. We didn't argue so much. No more than any couple you've ever known. I don't know the reason. Apart from this I don't feel any different to anyone else.

Your Dad's downstairs Josie. What will he need?

JOSIE. A cup of tea.

FAY. Go on then.

JOSIE *is moving into memory.* FAY *watches her.*

Can you see him?

JOSIE (*seeing it*). Yes.

FAY. What can you see?

JOSIE. I thought he was asleep on the sofa and he'd spilled something. I thought . . . what has he spilled? How can he sleep with that sticky mess on him?

The knife was sticking out of him like a handle.

And you were there after all. You were in the kitchen and you said behind me . . . 'Don't look at him pet . . . '

So I went to help you lay the table for breakfast. Got the cereal out the cupboard, put it on the table. Put the kettle on. Just like I always did on the days you were tired or cross. You were always up, dressed, your face washed. You couldn't light your own fags on mornings like that but you were always up for me.

And I'd set the table and put a mug of tea in front of you . . . and you'd say . . . you'd say . . .

FAY (*quiet, shaky*). There's my good girl . . . looking after her old Mum . . .

JOSIE. And today you said. 'He hurt me terribly you know. Terribly.' . . . And I heard him make a little noise, like a sigh . . . but you said . . . 'Don't look . . . '

FAY. No. Look at him Josie. Look at him.

JOSIE. So we drank our tea. Then Gran came in with her key . . .
and started screaming . . .

Pause.

FAY. We had a row. I don't remember what about . . . but after
we'd stopped he was fine and I was raging. We'd had a few
but not that many, enough so I can never remember all of it.

I was just sitting, just sitting in my chair like a coal burning
in the fire, so full of anger I couldn't move. I felt like I was
scorching my own clothes but I never made a sound. He
said 'Ach there's no talking to you . . . ' So he didn't.
He drank a beer. He watched a bit of television. He read
the paper and laughed at the sports news . . .

I just sat.

Once he looked at me and sort of snorted through his nose
in disgust. 'Aren't you going to bed?' he said.

I said nothing. I just sat. Burning.

He had another beer. He fell asleep and snored with the
telly lighting up his face, mouth open.

I sat and looked at him.

I felt that no-one could ever waste so much love on anyone.

I felt so full of crying that I was just tight with tears, from
my toes to my hair, stretched tight with crying that wouldn't
come out. I sat there for hours and I remembered. And what
I remembered, what I couldn't stop remembering, was a
moment when we are arguing when my anger flashed over
and started to burn me alive and that was the moment he
laughed at me. He set me on fire and watched me burn and
he laughed.

Then the strangest thing happened. I felt my lips pull back
from my teeth in a snarl like a dog's. I tried to close my
mouth but my lips kept twitching and tugging away from
my teeth. I bared my teeth like a wolf. Like a demon.
My eyes felt like they were popping out.

I felt there was a devil in me.

I felt I was the devil.

I think I was the devil then, or his dog.

I had a kitchen knife in my hand. I don't remember picking it up but it was in my hand.

I stuck it in him.

The stupid fuck, thinking he could just do or say anything he wanted and then snore away as if what he made me feel had no consequences at all. The stupid fuck.

You'd think he would've woken up more. Maybe we'd had more than I knew.

For two seconds I was glad when I saw him bleed. Then I just wished that none of it had ever happened at all.

I miss him so much. I miss him so much. I wish I'd never met him to hurt him so. You should remember your Dad. He loved you.

You should remember your Dad and go away from here and never come back.

JOSIE *is just frozen, staring at her.*

FAY (*advancing on her*). Go away! (*She starts shoving* JOSIE, *hitting her.*) Go away Josie! Leave me alone!

GUARD 1 *grabs* FAY.

Can you see him Josie!? Can you? Look at him! Look at what I did!

JOSIE. NO!

FAY (*pure venom*). Well you can still fuck off darling because you'll never bring me anything that's any good for me. You're fucking useless Josie! You can't even bring me a smoke!

JOSIE *turns on* FAY *lashing out at her.* GUARD 1 *is still holding* FAY. GUARD 2 *just watches as* JOSIE *hits her mother.*

GUARD 1. Sheila! SHEILA!

GUARD 2 *finally moves to intervene, restraining* JOSIE.

This visit is over! Do you understand me? This visit is over!

FAY. Yes. It's over.

Lights down.

GUARD 2 *is guiding* FAY *back to her room. She leads her in and lets her sit down. She is very gentle with her.*

GUARD 2. Alright Fay I think you've had enough. I think however you look at it you've had enough now haven't you?

FAY *doesn't respond.*

Let's get this room straightened up for you then shall we?

She clears up the wreck of the room quickly, sweeping away broken pictures, making the bed comfortable.

Do you want to just slip into bed now Fay?

FAY *shakes her head.*

Well I'll be back later with a cup of tea and a bourbon cream. How'll that be?

FAY (*very quiet*). Thanks Sheila.

GUARD 2 *leaves. Slow fade on* FAY *alone in her cell.*

Lights up on the interview room. JOSIE *is waiting. She looks quite different. She's wearing red. She has large earrings on, she looks as bright and sparkly as anyone could get away with, she's still on the right side of classy. She looks very good.*

GUARD 1 *comes in.*

GUARD 1. Josie isn't it?

JOSIE. That's right.

He holds out his hand, she shakes it.

GUARD 1. I knew it was Kerr but I couldn't remember the first bit. Never forget a face though. You're looking well.

JOSIE. Thank you. How are you?

GUARD 1. Oh overworked and under appreciated but that is the human condition for most of us isn't it Josie?

JOSIE. How has she been? Has she been O.K?

GUARD 1. She had a bad few months, I won't deceive you, she was very low but she seems much more herself these days.

JOSIE. Good.

GUARD 1. I don't know how she'd feel about a visit though and I have to say I'd wait a while before we brought that one up . . .

JOSIE *(cutting in)*. No. I don't want to visit her. I just wanted to let you know what the arrangements are.

GUARD 1. Right you are.

JOSIE. Someone from the solicitor's office will visit once a month. They can take a list of anything she wants and then that'll be brought in the next month. There's enough money in her name to pay for anything she's allowed. She can't have much can she? She'd probably like some new clothes . . . cigarettes.

GUARD 1. Well it's very good of you Josie. She'll appreciate that. It's very hard for women in here if there's no-one on the outside looking out for them.

JOSIE. I can't really do that. I can't visit her.

GUARD 1. No-one would expect you to, You didn't need to come in today you know. A letter would have been enough.

JOSIE. I know.

I wanted to thank you.

GUARD 1. Not necessary Josie.

JOSIE. You tried to warn me didn't you? I wanted to say thanks to you, and to your colleague as well I suppose . . .

GUARD 1. Sheila.

JOSIE. Yes.

GUARD 1. I shall certainly pass that on. Have you been keeping alright yourself?

JOSIE. Yes I'm . . . Well you know I had to change jobs . . .

GUARD 1. I hear a lot of things Josie. I only remember what's relevant to the job.

JOSIE (*smiles*). Thanks. Well, yeah, I got a new job, in Aberdeen. Gone home really, well where I was brought up. Where my Mum, my Gran lived. Felt like I wanted to settle down a bit, make a proper life for myself . . .

GUARD 1. Sounds good.

JOSIE. I mean my life was mad before.

GUARD 1. Everyone needs roots.

JOSIE. Yes. Anyway. Thanks.

GUARD 1. You're very welcome.

JOSIE *goes to leave, she turns back.*

JOSIE. Do you know, I'm sorry to be staring at you but you have always given me the strangest feeling every time I've met you. Do you know who you remind me of? Your mouth is the exact shape my Dad's was.

GUARD 1. I usually get Sean Connery. Not really. Your Dad's mouth you say? Well, everyone's related if you take it far enough back aren't they?

JOSIE. Yeah, I suppose you're right.

GUARD 1. Good-looking man your father I take it?

JOSIE. Yes. Yes he was, when he smiled . . . I have this really vivid memory of him . . . They were having a party down-stairs, him and Mum and some of the neighbours I think . . . I must've sneaked out of bed to see what the noise was.

I was standing in the doorway looking into the room and Dad was dancing Mum around, they were having such a good time . . . And Gran was sitting on the settee all squint with a can in her hand and she shouts out . . . 'Jim! Jim! there's that bairn out her bed and it's gone two in the morning!' And he turned and saw me. And his whole face lit up, like I was the one thing he wanted to make it a real party. And he let Mum go and he came and picked me up and then he made me put my feet on top of his feet. And we danced round the room together like that, together.

GUARD 1. That's a nice memory to have.

JOSIE. It's something eh?

Lights down on JOSIE *and* GUARD 1.

FAY *and* GUARD 2 *are sitting in the garden together. They are smoking.*

FAY. You're being very polite around me these days Sheila.

GUARD 2. I'm always polite Fay.

FAY *snorts*.

Well we'll be spending a lot of time together Fay. No sense in arguing.

FAY. Maybe not.

GUARD 2. Nice to see you've put on some weight too.

FAY. Can't return the compliment Sheila, you've enough arse there to insulate a loft.

GUARD 2. And you'll be on lockdown if you don't watch yourself Missus.

FAY. How's your girl?

GUARD 2. Starts nursery next week.

FAY. Oh that's a big one.

GUARD 2. It is. It'll cut the childcare bill but I'm not ready to send her out into the world. I'm not. There's kids at that school with mothers in here.

FAY. Poor wee things.

GUARD 2. Poor wee junkies in training.

FAY. You're a hard bitch Sheila.

FAY *gets back to gardening.*

GUARD 2. Working on it every day.

FAY. You've got to let kids go sooner or later.

GUARD 2. I suppose.

FAY *busies herself with the plants a moment.*

FAY. I daren't think about it. I daren't think about it because if I do I can't believe she'll ever be happy. Do you think she'll be happy Sheila?

GUARD 2 *says nothing.*

She'll do alright.

GUARD 2 (*snorts*). Aye, she'll do alright. Don't you doubt it. That one'll always land on her feet, up to her knees in money most likely.

FAY. Do you think?

GUARD 2. Oh aye.

FAY. And you think she'll be happy?

Pause.

GUARD 2. I don't know. How would I know?

FAY. After all that's happened to her . . . ?

GUARD 2. You made it happen to her Fay.

FAY. I could've looked after her. Forget about punishing me. I was what she needed. I was all she had left.

Pause.

GUARD 2. You surprised me you know . . . I always thought maybe he hit you or . . . I didn't think it made it right but I always wondered if that was why?

FAY. No, he didn't. Did your man hit you?

GUARD 2. No.

FAY. But don't tell me he never made you that angry. I know he did.

GUARD 2. You can't get me again Fay. I would never stab anyone. I know I wouldn't and that's a big difference between us.

FAY. Is it?

GUARD 2. It is. It's the reason you get to sit in a warm cosy little room with all your meals brought to you and I've got to go off now and wash shite off the walls. And where's the justice in that Fay?

GUARD 2 gets up. She pats FAY *down, She finds a stone in her pocket.*

What's this? What are you stealing rocks for?

FAY. Rocks belong to anyone.

GUARD 2. Well what do you want it for? Breaking windows? Sharpening something maybe?

FAY. I just liked the colour of it.

GUARD 2 is walking FAY *back to her cell.*

GUARD 2. Och don't tell me you're thinking of topping yourself Fay 'cause I won't buy it.

Pause.

FAY. No. Of course not.

GUARD 2 (*gentle*). Just keeping your options open eh? Och well, what's life without choices?

GUARD 2 hands FAY *back the rock. She ushers* FAY *into her cell and closes the door.* FAY *alone in her cell. She just sits. After a moment we hear* GUARD 2 *singing. It echoes round the corridor outside. A door slams, then another, silence.*

Fade lights.